SEXUAL
IMMORALITY

Our Vision

Called to bring the supernatural power of God to this generation.

Sexual Immorality

Edition 2018

Originally published in Spanish, under the title:
"La Inmoralidad Sexual"

ISBN: 978-1-59272-734-6

All rights reserved by **King Jesus International Ministry**

Project Director: Andres Brizuela
Spanish Editor: Jose M. Anhuaman
Translation to English: Gloria Zura
Cover Design: Juan Salgado
Interior Design: Jose M. Anhuaman

Category: Inner Healing

King Jesus International Ministry
14100 SW 144 Ave. - Miami, FL 33186
Tel: (305) 382-3171 - Fax: (305) 675-5770

Printed in the United States of America

SEXUAL IMMORALITY

Discover the steps to prevent bad thoughts and live with a pure mind

GUILLERMO MALDONADO

ACKNOWLEDGEMENTS

I am grateful to God because He saw me and chose me to serve Him. I am also grateful to my wife and children because they have been there for me unconditionally. I thank the Holy Spirit because He is the one revealing to me the will of God for my life and ministry. Also, I am grateful for all those people He has placed in my path to fulfill His mission. Thanks to all those who, in one way or another, have participated in the deliverance of many sons and daughters of God who were tied by the enemy's lies.

INDEX

INTRODUCTION 9

Chapter 1

The Battle of the Mind and Sexual Immorality 13

Chapter 2

Sexual Immorality and Demons 27

Chapter 3

Ten Most Common Illicit Sexual Practices 41

Chapter 4

Sexual Abuse 73

Chapter 5

Sex inside marriage 83

Chapter 6

Sanctification, the Solution to Sexual Problems 103

About the Author 117

Bibliography 119

INTRODUCTION

Sexual immorality is something almost no one speaks of, much less in the church or families in general, although we know it is a much-needed conversation to have. When we mention acts of sexual immorality, we are talking about masturbation, homosexuality, promiscuity, incest, abuse, adultery, fornication, bestiality, sexual fantasies; but also about pornography and watching obscene television programs, among many other things.

All these illicit practices wear down a person's resistance. They destroy homes and the fundamental institutions of society; they subdue men and women; adults, young people and children of all races and social stratum; they consume the foundations of the world and destroy entire nations.

Sexual Immorality: An Attitude of the Heart

According to Jesus' teachings, sexual impurity is an attitude of the heart, which begins before an individual starts acting immorally.

*You have heard that it was said to those of old, 'You shall not commit adultery.' But I say to you that whoever looks at a woman to lust for her has already committed adultery with her in his heart. —*MATTHEW *5:27-28*

Maybe many people have felt or feel today the desire of acting immorally, but they do not do it for several reasons. Nevertheless, according to the Scriptures, the sole act of entertaining dirty thoughts and desires counts as sin, just as if they had been executed.

Soul Ties

When the physical act is consummated, the result is a soul tie; and this is deeper and more dangerous than people think it is.

Referring to this matter, Apostle Paul says, *"Or do you not know that he who is joined to a harlot is one body with her? For "the two," He says, "shall become one flesh"* (1 Corinthians 6:16.)

When the sexual act is consummated, the bodies involved are joined. During this process, a soul tie is produced. There are good and bad soul ties. Good soul ties are based in love and produced inside marriage, because God's purpose is for man and woman to be united and be *"one flesh"* (Ephesians 5:31). Bad ties are perversions of the good and holy things, because they are founded upon lust. Bad soul ties are produced by sexual relations outside of marriage, and cause all spirits and bad influences to pass from one person to the other.

The worst part of all is that there are many married people, both men and women, that bring contamination to their homes and families because of the spiritual influences that they brought in via those illicit relations. That is why it is urgent that someone who has committed adultery, fornication or any other immoral sexual act be ministered in deliverance and inner healing.

Apostle Paul is so severe towards sexual immorality that he addresses the Ephesians in a rather radical manner saying, *"But fornication and all uncleanness or covetousness, let it not even be named among you, as is fitting for saints"* (Ephesians 5:3).

I know of cases in which a person who has fallen into sexual sin is disciplined by their leaders or pastors, which is the right thing to do, but he or she is not ministered in deliverance. This is just like taking out the spider web but leaving the spider behind to continue making webs in the same place. When these people are later put back into the positions they had before, it is almost inevitable for them to fall back into sin again. The reason they fall back is because they were never truly free from the root of the problem. That is why it is, in such cases, essential to minister a deep deliverance to these people.

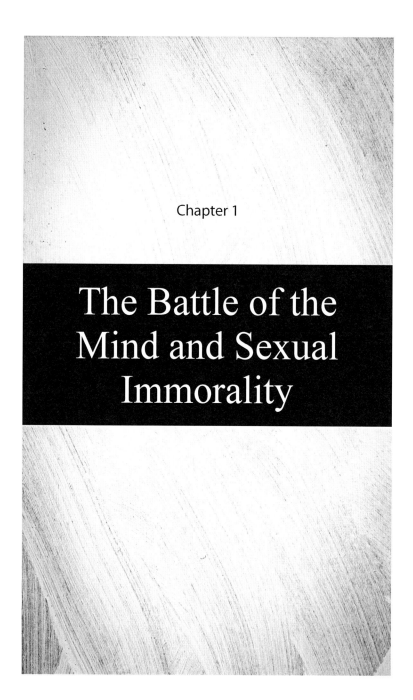

Chapter 1

The Battle of the Mind and Sexual Immorality

For centuries, the church has remained outside certain matters, but the greatest taboo that has always existed is sexual immorality. That is precisely why most people's problems and sins are related to sexual matters, in one way or another. Although the Word of God teaches us a lot about sex, people continue to perish because of their lack of knowledge.

At home, most parents don't know how to speak to their children about sex. Sooner or later, the children are either wrongly taught by their friends or learn to accept liberal and sinful sexual ideas. However, today, with the help of God, we will begin to learn about this fundamental topic, and answer some of the most frequent questions about sex.

What is Sex?

Sex is not bad. It was created by God; therefore, it is good as long as it is practiced with the purpose for which He created it. The purpose of this "good" sex is to bear fruit, multiply, fill the earth, subjugate it, and dominate over all of creation (see Genesis 1:27-28).

How Do Sexual Sins Begin?

Sexual sins begin in the mind of man, when man decides to disobey God and use sex for intentions different than the original divine purpose He had.

For example, nobody decides to suddenly commit adultery. A seed is first planted in the form of a bad thought which begins to grow in the human mind until it bears fruit in time. Many times, it begins with an innocent and kind action; but what begins well will end badly if it is not corrected in time.

In the parable of the wheat and the tares (Matthew 13:24-30), Jesus taught His disciples about a man who sowed a good seed in his field. The seed grew, but alongside it grew the tares as well. When the man was asked how it happened, he answered that the enemy had sowed the bad seed overnight.

But while men slept, his enemy came and sowed tares among the wheat and went his way. But when the grain had sprouted and produced a crop, then the tares also appeared.
—Matthew 13:25-26

This is an example of the enemy sowing a bad thought in people's minds, and it is strongest when they are at their most vulnerable; like when they are on bad terms in with their spouses, or when they are feeling lonely, or when they are needing the emotional support they are not getting at home, and other times of emotional crisis.

The night represents a moment of great weakness. This is the moment when the enemy plants a seed in the form of a bad thought. The bad seed begins to grow alongside the good seed. Suddenly, one glance from another person, one physical touch, one word of encouragement or a simple flattery, activates the carnal and sensual desire which is then transformed into action. In order to avoid reaching that moment, we must be attentive to what the Holy Spirit is telling and warning us about.

In the Old Testament, for a woman to be accused of infidelity she had to be caught in the act and this had to be confirmed by witnesses (Numbers 5:13). However, in the New Testament, Jesus teaches us that *"…whoever looks at a woman to lust for her has already committed adultery with her in his heart"* (Matthew 5:28.)

This means that if a man or a woman deliberately meditates or imagines himself or herself in a situation of adultery with a particular person, the sin of immorality has already been consummated in their heart – even if the external or physical sin has not actually been committed. Maybe your imagination has led you to visualize yourself kissing someone, being with them in an intimate situation, or some other sexual fantasy. Meditating continually around those kinds of thoughts automatically means that in your heart you have already committed adultery with that person.

Jesus illustrates this principle in a very simple way: sexual immorality is as a seed sowed in someone's mind in the form of a bad thought. If we let it grow, it will inevitably bear its fruits. This is dangerous. If we do not reject it the seed grows and in due time, we will reap its harvest, which are the terrible consequences sin brings with it.

It is not sinful to be tempted with sexual thoughts, but it is sin to entertain them.

We cannot keep birds from flying over our heads, but we can keep them from nesting and laying eggs inside our minds. The Bible refers to those bad thoughts as "viper's eggs", which the enemy deposits in our minds; but only if we allow him.

They hatch vipers' eggs and weave the spider's web; he who eats of their eggs dies, and from that which is crushed a viper breaks out. —ISAIAH 59:5

17

How to Avoid or Overcome Bad Thoughts

Bad thoughts can be avoided or overcome only by filling our minds with the peace of God. Philippians 4:7 says, *"And the peace of God, which surpasses all understanding, will guard your hearts and minds through Christ Jesus."* Likewise, 2 Corinthians 10:5 encourages us to bring *"every thought into captivity to the obedience of Christ."*

As we stop thinking as God thinks, we begin to nest thoughts of evil in our minds.

Temptation is a cycle of various circumstances that include:

- Attraction
- Seduction
- Conception
- Consummation
- Death

The Scripture says,

Blessed is the man who endures temptation; for when he has been approved, he will receive the crown of life which the Lord has promised to those who love Him. Let no one say when he is tempted, "I am tempted by God"; for God cannot be tempted by evil, nor does He Himself tempt anyone. But each one is tempted when he is drawn away by his own desires and enticed.
—JAMES 1:12 14

If an individual is attracted by his or her own lust or desire, they will feel seduced and will begin to play with bad thoughts, instead of rejecting them and taking them captive. These thoughts will then set up camp in their minds, and sin will be conceived by them. This stage may be called "pregnancy" –up to this moment physical sin has not been committed. Then, the "consummation" stage is reached, which includes the physical act.

Throughout my experience in the ministry, I have found a common denominator among people who have fallen into adultery, fornication or other sexual sins. That common denominator is the practice of their playing with that sin in their minds and hearts far before the consummation of the immoral act. That is how they opened the doors for the enemy to send temptations to them; tempting that had entered their minds in the form of thoughts. However, there are still several stages that occur before the physical act materializes.

What Happens if We Play with Sexually Immoral Thoughts?

- Immoral attraction in the mind begins to undermine the barriers of holiness.

- It destroys the barriers of morality and fear of the Lord.

- It builds barriers that separate us from our intimacy with God.

After all this, the person accepts immoral attraction and conceives it; which then becomes a sin in the mind and in the heart.

Testimony: This is the case of a man of God. He had a great ministry reaching thousands of people through radio and television. Sadly, one day, that minister committed adultery. This case illustrates very well what we have been explaining, because sin did not begin in the instant of the actual sexual act. Several years before, he had already sinned in his mind and heart; and because he was attracted and seduced, he conceived the sin and, finally, consummated it.

The most important thing man has is his heart. God created the heart of man so that out of it would spring life; but we must preserve it because bad things can also come out of it.

Keep your heart with all diligence, for out of it spring the issues of life. —PROVERBS 4:23

Jesus says to us: "It is not the food that contaminates man; it is not what is outside but what comes out of the heart." Many people think that as long as they do not perform the sexual act they are not sinning. They think playing and entertaining bad thoughts is not a sin. However, popular wisdom even says that if you play with fire, sooner or later, you will get burned.

How Should a Believer Think?

Do you think we honor God when we fill our minds with sexual fantasies of adultery and fornication? What about thoughts of greed, theft, revenge, homicide, judgement, bitterness, arrogance, lust, and folly? Of course not! All of that is sin against God.

How should a believer think? We must think as Jesus did, and we must know where all the bad things come from. Mark 7:21 says that, *"for from within, out of the heart of men, proceed evil thoughts, adulteries, fornications, murders."*

When some of the above mentioned exists in our hearts, the enemy will come to tempt us. The way he usually does so is by activating those bad thoughts and desires, so that we may fall into sin. Let us analyze in detail what Mark 7:21-23 says according to the Amplified Bible.

For from within, [that is] out the heart of men, come base and malevolent thoughts and schemes, acts of sexual immorality, thefts, murders, adulteries, acts of greed and covetousness, wickedness, deceit, unrestrained conduct, envy and jealousy, slander and profanity, arrogance and self-righteousness and foolishness (poor judgment). All these evil things [schemes and desires] come from within and defile and dishonor the man.

Then, what should we think about?

In his letter to the Philippians, Paul teaches us to think of *"whatever things are true, whatever things are noble, whatever things are just, whatever things are pure, whatever things are lovely, whatever things are of good report, if there is any virtue and if there is anything praiseworthy—meditate on these things"* (Philippians 4:8).

What the apostle is telling us is that we should take responsibility for every thought and action. It urges us to fixate our minds on every one of the virtues previously cited. Just knowing that the result we will get from doing that will bring peace to our minds and into our hearts.

The Old Testament says, *"You will keep him in perfect peace, whose mind is stayed on You, because he trusts in You."* (Isaiah 26:3) while the New Testament validates the same when it declares, *"And the peace of God, which surpasses all understanding, will guard your hearts and minds through Christ Jesus"* (Philippians 4:7).

God is not only interested in what we do, but also in what we think.

Up until now we have had a wrong conception of sin because we believe that it is only wrong when we do evil things or commit the sin itself. Although that is not an entirely wrong way to believe, the Scripture is clear when it says that, *"the word of God is living and powerful, and sharper than any two-edged sword, piercing even to the division of soul and spirit, and of joints and marrow, and is a discerner of the thoughts and intents of the heart"* (Hebrews 4:12.)

God expects our lives to be pure. Why then does so much sin exist in churches and in the world? It is because our minds are contaminated with thoughts that lead us to sin. The atmosphere surrounding us is constantly bombarding our minds with thoughts and images that stimulate us to sin. Those images are most commonly presented in television, cinema, publicity, and in every other channel of media out there. That is why we are the way we are!

It is awful to see marriages destroyed, children become rebellious because of divorce, believers go astray because someone hurt them or because they entertained bad thoughts instead of cutting them off in time. He who commits a sexual sin does it because, much before the consummation, he had conceived it in his mind and heart.

An individual who accepts a bad thought in his mind, does so believing he will never reach the point of consummation; but nothing can be further from the truth. The truth is that when the devil presents him with an opportunity, that individual will commit the sin easily because he had already accepted it in his mind.

As we mentioned earlier, every person that has fallen into sexual sin confesses to have accepted a thought related to that sin, several months or years before. Besides that, each one of them thought they had it under control. The same thing happens to alcohol or drug addicts. They say, "I can stop at any time," but the truth is they cannot.

How to Prevent Sin and Stop Oneself from Walking into Death?

Therefore, since Christ suffered for us in the flesh, arm yourselves also with the same mind, for he who has suffered in the flesh has ceased from sin, that he no longer should live the rest of his time in the flesh for the lusts of men, but for the will of God. —1 PETER 4:1-2

> **Jesus took the sin of humanity as His own, and gave us victory over evil thoughts.**

Arm yourself then with that thought. Because Jesus died for us and triumphed over sin and death, it is possible to live free from evil thoughts! We no longer need to be dominated nor controlled by them! The word Peter uses is "arm" because when we "arm ourselves with" or "adopt" Jesus' thoughts, they become powerful arms of war according to the Amplified Bible translation, which says,

"Therefore, since Christ suffered in the flesh [and died for us], arm yourselves [like warriors] with the same purpose [being willing to suffer for doing what is right and pleasing God], because whoever has suffered in the flesh [being like-minded with Christ] is done with [intentional] sin [having stopped pleasing the world]." —1 PETER 4:1

Steps to Prevent Bad Thoughts from Coming In

We must learn to handle our thoughts. We cannot let ourselves be controlled nor seduced by them because we are the fruit of our thoughts. That what we think will truly reach our hearts; and from the abundance of the heart our mouth shall speak; and our acts will be based upon the same.

Hear, O earth! Behold, I will certainly bring calamity on this people— The fruit of their thoughts, because they have not heeded My words nor My law, but rejected it. —JEREMIAH 6:19

The following are the most important steps to prevent bad thoughts from coming in:

1. **Cut the cycle and repent.** Every person who wants to please God must break the cycle of evil thoughts they may have been allowing in their minds and start changing their mentality. Also, they must recognize every unclean thought of hate, vengeance, judgement, theft, greed, adultery, and fornication, and repent for them.

2. **Activate a cycle of new thoughts.** Once you have cut the cycle of evil thoughts, you must activate a cycle of good thoughts or a new way of thinking that will lead you to please God. In all of this, you must be aware that the Lord knows our every thought.

   The Lord knows the thoughts of man, that they are futile. —PSALMS 94:11

   It is not easy to keep ourselves in the spirit because the world is continually attacking our minds; therefore, doing so requires a big effort. To be able to achieve this you must leave behind everything that leads you to sin. Remember, it is impossible to defeat evil thoughts in our own strength.

We must ask the Holy Spirit for help and make a solid decision to renounce them.

3. **Make a covenant with God to keep your mind pure and clean.** To be able to achieve this it is important for you to have in mind the following questions: What kind of thoughts have you been entertaining in your mind? Have they been unclean thoughts of judgement, vengeance, wrath, or hate? If the answer to any of these questions is "yes," the first thing you must do is to repent and make a covenant with God to keep your mind clean and pure from now on. Do it right now!

4. **Bring every thought into captivity**

   Casting down arguments and every high thing that exalts itself against the knowledge of God, bringing every thought into captivity to the obedience of Christ.
   —2 Corinthians 10:5

Every time those thoughts come to your mind, do not entertain them! Command them to leave right away!

When an evil thought comes into your mind, bring it into captivity and replace it with a good thought. The Word of God commands us to think about everything that is good, kind, and of good report. In everything that is holy, the Scripture says, "meditate on these things."

SYNOPSIS

- Immorality is an attitude of the heart.

- Many sexual sins begin with the sowing of a seed in the mind in the form of a thought. The enemy will sow an evil thought in the moment of lowest spiritual resistance or greatest weakness.

- Once that thought becomes a physical act, there will be an inevitable soul tie.

- Jesus said that we must not entertain or play with evil thoughts because when we do so, adultery has already been committed in the heart.

- The way to eliminate evil thoughts is bringing them into captivity to the obedience of Christ.

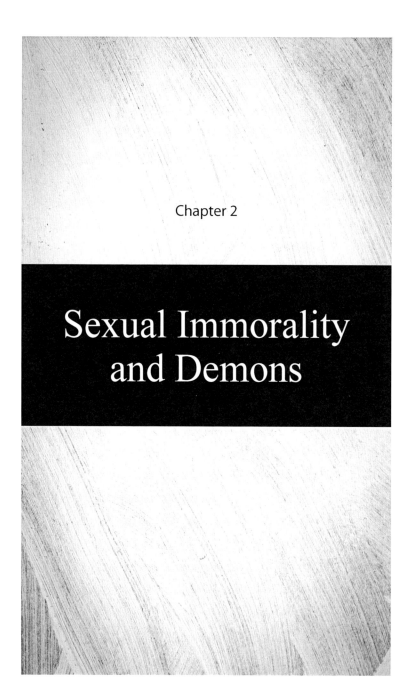

Chapter 2

Sexual Immorality and Demons

*I*n my experience ministering deliverance to men, I have found that on average, seven out of ten men face sexual problems in silence. Sadly, this is one of the topics least spoken about in church; yet, at the same time, it is one of the most common sins that abound in churches.

Speaking about the works of the flesh, Apostle Paul begins with sins related to the body. This kind of sin is responsible for many destroyed families in the church of Christ; but more so, it is the underlying cause of many of today's devastated ministries, including those nearing extinction.

Sexual Sins or Sexual Impurity

According to the letter sent to the Galatians, there are four sexual sins from which the others derive. These sins are: adultery, fornication, filthiness, and lust.

1. Adultery

The word "adultery" comes from the Greek term moiheia, which refers to the action of having sexual relations with another person outside of marriage.

Adultery is a sin of the flesh that trespasses or violates the biblical principles set by God. In the past and up until today, this sin has propagated itself as an epidemic in the body of Christ and in the world. Thus, we can see how ministers and entire ministries, some of which have been exposed to a greater degree than others, that have been destroyed because of this. We, as a church, must talk clearly about this problem and confront it effectively in order to be able to prevent it from continuing to happen as well as to have a healthy and pure people before God.

The Bible shows us four types of adultery:

- **Adultery in the eyes.** The lust in the eyes is one of the main roots of sin. This is the reason Job made a covenant with his eyes, to not look at a virgin woman with lust. The translation from the Amplified Bible says in Job 31:1, *"I have made a covenant (agreement) with my eyes; how then could I gaze [lustfully] at a virgin?"* Let us remember that temptations come to men, first, through the sense of sight. That is why men must have conviction of sin, and decide to make a covenant to look at a woman with nothing but purity.

- **Adultery in the heart.** According to the Word of God, it is not sinful to look at a woman and admire her beauty, as long as there is purity in the heart of the beholder. However, it is a sin to look upon a woman lustfully. When lust comes into a man's mind, he has already committed sin in his heart.

  You have heard that it was said to those of old, 'You shall not commit adultery.' —MATTHEW 5:27

- **Adultery in the mind.** There are people who play frequently with illicit sexual thoughts. If anybody has those kind of sexual fantasies, it is as if he or she had already committed the sin. In fact, every time they entertain those kind of thoughts, in their minds they are sinning.

■ **Adultery in the body.** This is the consummation of a sin. It is the physical doing of something that first entered through the eye, and was then entertained in the mind, meditated upon, and, finally, conceived.

Adultery in the body is the practical realization of what had started as a thought.

It is important to emphasize that these four types of adultery begin with a thought. If that thought is entertained, it pollutes the heart, the eyes, and the body.

2. Fornication

Fornication comes from the Greek word porneia –which is the word pornography comes from. This term refers to a sexual relation between two people that are not married. Whatever way you look at it, this is an illicit relation; even if they have lived together for a long time.

Churches nowadays have a great deal of people among their members who are living together and have children together but are not married. That is why the blessings of God have not come to their homes in full. Why do these people not want to get married? Most of them do not want to get married because they do not want to commit themselves. They think, "If this union does not work out, I'll leave and look for another partner." Thus, they are always looking for the ideal person here and there; meanwhile, they are living with someone, despite knowing they are sinning against God.

You may have lived with the same person for twenty years and may even have had four children with that person, but the truth is that if you are not married to that person, you are in fornication; and that is a sin of the flesh that God severely punishes.

As we saw before, once two people become sexually united, physical, emotional, and spiritual ties occur. But besides that, a transfer of spirits also occurs. This happens because, in the moment of deepest intimacy, they become one flesh and their souls melt together. In deliverance language, this is known as "soul tie." That is why people that commit adultery or fornication find it so hard to separate from each other; because a part of their soul stays tied to (or becomes impregnated with) the soul of their partner. That is the reason why divorces are so painful for both people involved.

As much as those who live in adultery or fornication try desperately to leave sin, they find it very difficult to do so in their own strength. Somebody has to help them because they have fallen into a trap of the enemy from which it is too hard to escape–if not seemingly impossible.

Adultery is a sin that comes from the heart, and it is highly contaminating.

What is the attitude of a person who is living in adultery or fornication? They say and believe, "Nobody can see me!" Let us remember that even when no one sees us in earth, there is One who does see everything from Heaven, and that One is God.

The eye of the adulterer waits for the twilight, saying, 'No eye will see me'; and he disguises his face. —JOB 24:15

What is the attitude we should have towards people who live in adultery or fornication? The best is to be parted from them.

But now I have written to you not to keep company with anyone named a brother, who is sexually immoral, or covetous, or an idolater, or a reviler, or a drunkard, or an extortioner—not even to eat with such a person… "put away from yourselves the evil person." —1 CORINTHIANS 5:11, 13

All in all, we must say that sins of adultery and fornication are an abomination before the eyes of the Lord; that is why we need to be separated from them.

3. Uncleanness

In a broad sense, the word uncleanness means dirtiness, filth, or trash. The Merriam Webster Dictionary defines it as "morally or spiritually impure."

In the sexual immorality field, it is considered the lowest of all the sexual sins. Uncleanness is a moral blind spot that characterizes people given to lust and sexual debauchery. It is a combination of adultery, fornication, masturbation, homosexuality, lesbianism, and incest, among other aberrations.

Woe to you, scribes and Pharisees, hypocrites! For you are like whitewashed tombs which indeed appear beautiful outwardly, but inside are full of dead men's bones and all uncleanness. —MATTHEW 23:27

4. Lust

Lust comes from the Greek word *aselgeia*, indicating excess, lack of restraint, indecency, lack of self-control, licentiousness, and dissolution (laxity of costumes). It is one of the evils that come from the heart.

Who, being past feeling, have given themselves over to lewdness, to work all uncleanness with greediness.
—EPHESIANS 4:19

The term aselgeia also means lust, shameless indecency, concupiscence, and unlimited depravation.

Lust is to commit a sin in plain daylight, for everyone to see, with arrogance and insolence.

As we can see, these sins get progressively graver. A sin of lust occurs when the person has reached such lack of restraint that he or she cannot stop themselves from committing those acts, and they do them shamelessly. In such cases, the person lives with total lack of control, lack of decency, and becomes filthy in every aspect.

Lust not only refers to the sexual area, it also includes any area of our lives that has lack of restraint; for example, when you eat too much, there is lust in your mouth. Those who abuse drugs fall into a cycle of lust because they cannot satisfy their addiction; and this happens with any other sin, as long as a person reaches the point of lack of restraint.

This manner of sinning without restraint doesn't merely appear at the beginning, rather it is a process in which an individual progressively loses control and restraint over their thoughts, body and life. When a sin is committed continually, doors are opened for many demons to come and oppress that person; and for every work of the flesh, there is a demon that torments those who practice these works.

> *When a person falls in lust he or she has already lost the fear of the Lord.*

These are the individuals who end up becoming rapists, child abusers, and people who commit uncontrolled abominations. They become involved in the dirtiest and most violent sexual practices, only to satisfy their compulsive desires. Lust destroys everything around us, especially our marriages and families. Only Jesus can set them free from that form of slavery. Sexual sins occur in church more frequently than anybody can imagine. There are men who attend church and sexually covet some women of the congregation. Likewise, there are women full of seductive spirits whose only purpose is to seduce men of God.

Where Do Sexual Sins Come from?

- **Generational curses.** These are the most common causes for sexual immorality to come into a person's life. With more than two decades in ministry, I have found that many of the sexual problems that the present generation faces follow a pattern set by their ancestors. In other words, the problems that challenge men and women of these times come from their parents and grandparents, and these problems will continue until someone breaks that curse. The Bible says God visits the iniquity of the fathers to the third and fourth generation of those who hate Him (Deuteronomy 5:9). Without a doubt, this is a curse inheritance.

- **Sexual oppressions of the past.** Sexual immorality can also come through traumas, incest, and all kinds of abuses and violations the person has suffered or were committed in his past.

- **Pornography.** In today's world, a major part of the Media uses some ingredients of pornographic content. This content attacks our minds, affects our will, and undermines our moral values.

Testimony: There is a young man who would spend day and night watching pornography. He tells us he could watch up to six movies in one day, and when he finished them he would go to his room and masturbate. One night he woke up at 2:00 am to masturbate, but was suddenly overcome with a conviction of sin and said, "God, I can't do this anymore!" He began crying like a child. When he reached out for help at church, he was delivered. Then, he says that one day he took all those videos he had at home, put them in a bag, and threw them away where nobody could pick them up. Today that man is thankful to God because He broke that curse in his life.

How to Stay Away from Sexual Sins

What is the solution for sexual sins? What can a Christian do if he or she has problems with lust, adultery, fornication, uncleanness, pornography, lesbianism, or homosexuality?

Every sexual sin can be prevented by taking every thought into captivity to the obedience of Christ.

There are two main things we can do:

- **Find out the causes.** Investigate if sexual immorality is caused by a demonic spirit influence. How do you know that? The best way is by examining if the problem is becoming a compulsive desire, meaning that you cannot control it. If you have tried breaking the cycle of sin in prayer and fasting but have not been able to do so, then you must reach out be ministered in deliverance. God will set you free.

If the problem is due to the works of the flesh, prayer, fasting, and a life set aside for the Lord will give you the power to control anything that may be affecting you. The best advice is to live by crucifying the flesh day after day.

- **Flee from sin.** Temptations and sexual sins cannot be resisted or rebuked. Do not wait until they come. Do not entertain them in your mind. Do not play around with them. Run away! Try not to stay alone with a person of the opposite sex. Get married instead of falling into fornication.

But I say to the unmarried and to the widows: It is good for them if they remain even as I am; but if they cannot exercise self-control, let them marry. For it is better to marry than to burn with passion. —1 CORINTHIANS 7:8-9

I have found many people that say, "Pastor, I am strong and can resist sexual temptation," and they stay instead of fleeing. The result is that they end up falling into sin. Let us see the case of Joseph in the Bible.

But it happened about this time, when Joseph went into the house to do his work, and none of the men of the house was inside, that she caught him by his garment, saying, "Lie with me." But he left his garment in her hand, and fled and ran outside. —GENESIS 39:11-12

When you flee temptations, you have advantage.

If you try to face temptations and entertain them, they become ten times stronger. If you know there are things that have an influence on you or that lead you to sin, take drastic measures, like parting completely from certain friends, places, and situations. Apostle Paul says,

Flee sexual immorality. Every sin that a man does is outside the body, but he who commits sexual immorality sins against his own body. —1 CORINTHIANS 6:18

There are people who cannot untie themselves from sin. Other people do not want to do so because they like it. If this is your case, I tell you beforehand you will not be free until you decide to let it go. If you truly want to stop offending God, I assure you that making the decision to flee rather than entertain sinful ideas, will allow God to begin setting you free, because as the Scripture says, "For this is the will of God, your sanctification: that you should abstain from sexual immorality" (1 Thessalonians 4:3.)

SYNOPSIS

- All sexual sins derive from: adultery, fornication, uncleanness, and lust.

- There are four types of adultery: in the eyes, in the heart, in the mind, and in the body.

- Adultery and fornication begin with one thought. It is not good to entertain evil thoughts.

- The three main causes of sexual sin are: generational curses, oppressions from the past, and pornography.

- We must investigate the causes that lead to sexual immorality.

- If it is an unclean spirit, reach out for deliverance.

- If it is a work of the flesh, crucify it and do not satisfy its desires.

- Flee all sexual sin. Do not entertain evil thoughts or stay in places where you can be tempted.

- Get married instead of living in fornication.

- The best advice: separate and run away from sexual sin, and look for deliverance before it is too late.

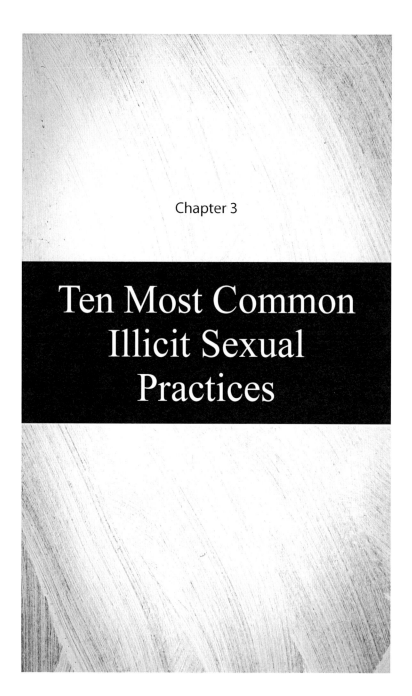

Chapter 3

Ten Most Common Illicit Sexual Practices

*I*n this chapter, we will share about the ten most common illicit sexual practices. One by one, we will study the origin and consequences of these sins, as well as share the appropriate biblical direction to overcome them.

1. MASTURBATION

Masturbation is the stimulation or manipulation of the genital organs or erogenous zones to give sexual pleasure. It is a habit formed to obtain sexual enjoyment in solidarity.

Masturbation usually begins at an early age and can be produced by a desire to stimulate oneself. It can also develop as a consequence of having suffered sexual abuse. Once the habit is established, it cannot be resisted, and it can continue well into adulthood. Often, this illicit sexual practice can continue even while the person is married.

The main spirit that operates in these cases is the spirit of lust. This spirit attacks and controls one sex as it attacks the other. Before we study whether a sin that is practiced continuously opens doors for an unclean spirit of lust to come in through, we must first make sure that this is in fact what happened. In cases such as these, it is harder to be set free, even though nothing is impossible to God.

How Does Masturbation Develop in People?

Masturbation develops in people in two ways:

- **By choice.** There are certain individuals who willfully choose to practice this vice; giving way to an evil spirit of addiction and lust.

- **By an inherited influence.** There are cases in which masturbation had been practiced by a parent or some other relatives, such as grandparents, great-grandparents, or other ancestors, and their descendants (their children) inherit this unclean desire.

Consequences of Masturbation

- Guilt, low self-esteem, spiritual infertility, and sometimes even divorce are the main consequences of practicing masturbation.

Sadly, some physicians, psychiatrists, psychologists, and counselors even recommend masturbation as a way to escape, as if it were not a sin. Yet it is a sin. It is lust and it is associated with sexual fantasies.

> *Masturbation is an*
> *egocentric practice.*

There are individuals that often reach the point of idolizing their own sexual organs. Such practice contradicts the biblical standards of purity completely. Also, it has been scientifically proven that masturbation negatively affects the prostate gland in men, causing physical dysfunctions in the sexual area.

The Solution to this Problem

There is a solution to this problem, I am glad to say, thanks to God! I have seen hundreds of people set free from this vice, from this spirit of lust, that led them to masturbation. However, for this to happen, there are some steps that must be followed:

- Repent before God.

- Renounce voluntarily.

- Renew the mind.

- Throw away magazines, videos, and every material with pornographic content.

- Do not play around with unclean thoughts about sex.

- Look for deliverance at church, with the pastor or the leaders.

Testimony: My problem was fornication and masturbation. I was married for a while in Cuba, but I never achieved anything good in my marriage because of my sin. My parents had taught me masturbation was normal, that it was a part of youth, and that way I would relieve some stress. On the other hand, a psychologist also told me that it was normal; so I never considered it a sin. I felt fine talking to my friends about all my adventures, but I was never able to find what everybody was looking for in life, which was inner peace and to follow truth. I was living in fornication and I would have given anything for just one moment of the happiness that only God can give us., but did not have.

My mother had given her life to the Lord and used to speak to me a lot about God. She would ask me to read the Bible for her, saying she was tired. I began to seek after the Lord and one day, while praying in bed, I began to speak in other tongues. I am thankful my mother had talked to me about tongues before because if she had not I would have thought I was going crazy. Then, I came to understand that "God is alive, not dead." I felt really touched by Him. This is not something that comes by chance, but rather something you look for. I told God, "Father, I know I need to urgently change my life" and He began to change me, little by little. One day I was tempted; I went to the Internet and found some emails offering me pornography. Even though I was used to this and thought it was normal before, this time I felt a voice saying, "Don't you know that demons can enter your house even through what seem like little things?"

Now I feel as good as a new person and I know what I want: a wife, a home, and to get ahead in life. God touched me and set me free. Fornication, pornography, and masturbation are the biggest diseases of today, even though our society thinks of them as meaningless "little things."

Testimony: Since I was a little girl I used to masturbate frequently because I had seen my parents having sexual relations; that traumatized me to the point that it stuck in my mind. I got married and continued to practice it, until we ended up divorcing. Eventually, I got together with another man but continued to masturbate. When I attended church, I began to feel the presence of God and the Holy Spirit begin to work in me. One night, I knelt down before the Lord and told Him that I didn't want to feel that way anymore. I asked Him to take that feeling away from me and He did! From that night on, I never felt the desire to masturbate again. I was free!

Testimony: I was tied by a spirit of masturbation and fornication. That spirit came into my life when I saw my mother committing adultery. I would fast and pray but there was never a break-through in my life; I continued with the same problem. Many time I cried out to the Lord, asking Him to take away that prob-lem because I wanted to praise Him in purity. Then I entered an-other fast and I saw Satan telling me, "You are mine. I am going to have sex with you," and I told him, "This time I won't fall! I won't"! The Holy Spirit led me to say, "I tie my body to Your throne, I tie my mind to Your Word, I tie my body to Your blood." When I said this, I heard a chain break and I heard the sound of a serpent. God set me free and gave me the revelation that I should use His Word to defeat temptation. Now Christ fills my heart more than sex, more than food, more than anything else. It is possible to be free!

Testimony: I used to look at pornographic magazines my dad kept in his closet, and that affected me in such a way that it stuck in my mind. Although I felt fear, I liked it. I felt myself attracted toward that material. I thought that whenever I wanted to leave masturbation I would be able to do so because I thought I had self-control. But to tell the truth, it was the other way around; masturbation had control over me. In fact, I would hear an inner voice telling me, "You are mine." I was desperate; and when someone is really desperate to be healed, God heals that individual. I asked God to heal me. One day, with the Bible in my hand, I said, "Forgive me Lord. You know this is stronger than I am. This is a fight between the devil and You. I cannot defeat it; only You can defeat it." When I said those words, God set me free. Now I feel free and I am happy!

2. INCEST AND SEXUAL ABUSE

The experiences of incest and sexual abuse are always devastating and cause short and long-term problems.

Consequences of these Sexual Problems

One of the main consequences of sexual problems, among many, is that the victim feels deceived. This makes a person emotionally cold and causes them to withdraw into themselves while with others. In the long term, when these people get married, they realize they are sexually frigid.

Victims of these kind of abuses often think that sex is dirty and cannot participate in it, not even within their marriage. They feel guilty and filthy. Every time they make love to their partner, they feel as if they are being tortured and that they have no other choice but to subject themselves to it, and to accept it. Then there are others who, because of this problem, become extremely lustful. Rather than holding back from it, they compulsively desire to have sex every day, and sometimes just one partner is not enough to satisfy them/

As a consequence, these individuals believe no decent person is ever going to accept them as a suitable partner in a serious formal relationship. The majority of these individuals who have been sexually abused or molested and up destroying their homes and even their own lives.

The Solution to these Problems

- **Deliverance.** You can achieve this by renouncing every spirit of incest, lust, frigidity, and abuse. If you cannot do it alone, ask for direction from a person who knows about deliverance so that you may be helped.

- **Inner healing for the emotions.** When an individual has been sexually abused, his or her soul gets fragmented (although we will later refer to this topic in more detail, for now we can briefly state that the soul is broken into pieces) and their emotions are hurt and their souls needs inner healing.

- **Forgive the abusers.** Forgiveness is the main key for a person to be free, healed, and restored. If the person does not forgive, God cannot do anything at all. He or she needs to wholeheartedly forgive.

- **Pray to clean the mind.** Only with a pure mind can one have the right attitude towards sex in marriage.

3. SEXUAL PROMISCUITY

Let us define some sexual acts that open doors for demonic spirits to come into our lives. We have studied some of them before and they are:

- **Fornication.** The sexual intercourse between two people without their being married to each other.

- **Adultery.** It is having sexual intercourse outside of their marriage. An act of infidelity.

- **Masturbation.** The stimulation of our own sexual organs as an act of lust, with the purpose of self-satisfaction. Some people practice masturbation as an alternative to the pleasure of a sexual relationship and to prevent the risk of pregnancy.

- **Oral sex.** It is the stimulation of the sexual organs by mouth, as an act of lust. The main reason oral sex is forbidden by the Word of God is because God created every organ of the human body to fulfill specific functions. God made the mouth for us to speak, feed ourselves, worship Him and bless Him; not to have sex. That goes against the nature established by God. That is why God created man and woman with sexual organs that fulfill those specific functions.

- **Sexual masochism practices.** A sexual perversion where violence and pain is used to obtain pleasure. This practice dishonors the body, perverts the nature of human relations, and offends God.

Consequences of Sexual Promiscuity

- **Spiritual, physical, and emotional death**

The man who commits adultery with another man's wife, he who commits adultery with his neighbor's wife, the adulterer and the adulteress, shall surely be put to death. —LEVITICUS 20:10

Although adultery has damaging temporal consequences, it also brings is well known to cause devastating eternal consequences. The destructive consequences in the natural (temporal) realm are sickness, poverty, and misery. There are also spiritual consequences, such as wounds, pain, devastation, and depression in the family.

- **Corruption or fragmentation of the soul**

The person who commits adultery or any other act of sexual promiscuity is blinded in his or her understanding by a spirit of deceit and lies. Therefore, he or she does not understand the damage he is bringing to his family, his children, and over the entire Kingdom of God.

Whoever commits adultery with a woman lacks understanding; he who does so destroys his own soul. —PROVERBS 6:32

The Bible says that he who commits adultery destroys his soul. Here the word "destroy" in Hebrew gives the idea of "fragmenting." When the soul suffers deep and violent pain, which happens when there is abuse or sexual immorality, the soul becomes fragmented. This means that the soul is divided or broken into pieces, thus, fragmented, and taken into captivity.

That is why the adulterer or sexually promiscuous person is unstable, confused, and never satisfied. He or she always feels incomplete and displeased with him or herself.

- **Wounds and dishonor or shame**

Wounds and dishonor he will get, and his reproach will not be wiped away. —Proverbs 6:33

The first ones to suffer emotional wounds are the members of your own family. There are many children with pain in their hearts because either their mom or dad left them to go with another person. The consequences are devastating. Some kids grow up with resentment, bitterness, and hate towards their parents. Others end up feeling rejection, loneliness, or become enslaved to drugs or other addictions. The saddest thing is knowing that when they grow up they will also commit adultery, because this is a curse that goes from one generation to the other.

Other consequences are the many wounds sowed in the heart of the spouses such as lack of forgiveness, bitterness, hate, and rancor, due to the betrayal and infidelity of the spouse who left them. This brings shame and dishonor in every area of their life.

The affront of adultery is never erased. Adultery is always present in the mind and hearts of those who suffered from it. It is as an indelible mark that will always be present in their lives. The Lord forgives and forgets, but the consequences of our failures remain forever.

Personally, I have prayed for many children whose parents got divorced due to sexual promiscuity. Most of them became involved with drugs, or fell into other addictions; many became part of gangs, and others died. That is why it is so important to appeal to the hearts of those parents that are today immersed in these kinds of practices; for them to reconsider what they are doing and repent for their sin; so that they may part from evil and return home. God will forgive them and restore them. There is still time if there is a genuine repentance. If you don't do that for yourself, do it for your family; but above all, do it for God.

- **They lose their inheritance in the Kingdom of God**

  ...Do not be deceived. Neither fornicators, nor idolaters, nor adulterers, nor homosexuals, nor sodomites, nor thieves, nor covetous, nor drunkards, nor revilers, nor extortioners will inherit the kingdom of God. —1 CORINTHIANS 6:9-10

  The Scripture tells us clearly that he or she who commits adultery cannot inherit the Kingdom of God unless he or she repents for their sin.

- **They will be judged by God**

  Marriage is honorable among all, and the bed undefiled; but fornicators and adulterers God will judge.
  —HEBREWS 13:4

  God is merciful and good with everybody, but those who do not repent for their sins, such as fornication and adultery, will be judged by God publicly. Those sins bring about shame and dishonor. Those who commit adultery can lose their family, because this is the only acceptable biblical reason to get divorced.

And I say to you, whoever divorces his wife, except for sexual immorality, and marries another, commits adultery; and whoever marries her who is divorced commits adultery. —Matthew 19:9

4. SEXUAL FANTASIES

Sexual fantasies can become so strong that they can dominate a person's mind, causing a loss of realistic awareness. Jesus warned us that man can fall into adultery even if the act has not been consummated.

Sexual fantasies speed up immoral activity.

Now, even though we already studied Matthew 5:28, we must do it in detail. The Amplified Bible Translation says,

But I say to you that everyone who [so much as] looks at a woman with lust for her has already committed adultery with her in his heart. —Matthew 5:28

This is the reason pornography, in any of its forms, must be avoided because it can lead to practices of sexual promiscuity and unclean acts of every kind. We cannot play around with sexual fantasies in our minds because of the many reasons that we have been studying up to now.

5. PORNOGRAPHY

The Greek word *pornographos* has its roots in the word porno which means prostitute, and includes everything related to

53

their job; and in the word *graphein* or *grapho* which means to engrave, write, or illustrate those activities. If we bring those meanings together, we can conclude that pornography is the representation of sexual acts in videos, X or R rated movies (of high sexual content), magazines, books, and the performance of live sex acts. Prostitution is the act by which a person willfully participates in the activities mentioned above in exchange for money.

Pornographic Industry Statistics

At 13.3 billion dollars, the revenues of the sex and pornography industry in the United States are bigger than those of the NFL, NBA, and MLB combined. According to This Top Ten Reviews report made by an investigative group (http://TopTenReviews. com/pornography) updated numbers from 2006 confirm that the sex industry sold 97 billion dollars' worth of content worldwide. To put this in perspective, Microsoft reported 44.8 billion dollars, and this company sells the most used operating computer systems in the world as well as other products.

China leads this industry, followed by South Korea, Japan, and the United States.

According to that report, every second:

- 28,258 users watch pornography on the Internet.

- $3,075.64 dollars are payed for pornography on the Internet.

- 372 people write the word "adult" in search engines.

Furthermore:

- Every 39 minutes a new pornographic video is produced in the USA.

- Every day 266 new porno sites are created on the Internet.

- Sundays are the days in which more pornography is consumed.

- 70% of the visits to porno sites on the Internet are produced between 9am and 5pm (working hours).

- 60% of all visits to the Internet are of sexual nature (Source: Survey of 2000 by MSNBC).

- 25% of all internet searches are related to pornography. This is equivalent to 68 million searches per day.

- 47% of American families say porn is a problem in their home.

- 35% of Internet downloads are pornographic.

- 25 million Americans spend between 1-10 hours per week in pornographic sites (Survey made in 2000 by MSNBC).

- 72% pornography consumers are men.

- 28% pornography consumers are women.

- Young people between the ages of 12 and 17 are the biggest consumers of pornography, according to http://www.enough.org/ based on governmental studies. This same study reports that:

- There are 1.5 billion pornographic downloads a month (35% out the total number of downloads).

- The global market of cyber porno is worth $4.9 billion.

- On the Internet, the porn industry has more profits than Microsoft, Google, Amazon, eBay, Yahoo, Apple, and Netflix combined.

- Only in the USA, pornography on the Internet produces more profits than the NFL, the major leagues of Baseball, and the NBA.

- According to the latest numbers published by http://listas.eleconomista.es/economia/240-las-industrias-que-mas-dinero-mueven-en-el-mundo, the 200 X cinema studios in the United States billed 60 billion dollars in 12 months, surpassing the entire Hollywood industry.

- Video and DVD rentals went from 450 million in 1992 to 800 million in 2002.

- A study named "El negocio de la pornografía" (The Pornography Business) that appears on the site http://www.uji.es./bin/publ/ediciones/jif9/publ/7.pdf estimates that at least one out of four regular internet users visit pornographic sites, with a minimum of once a month (Nielsen/NetRatings). This is more people than the people visiting sport and governmental sites put together.

- A report made by Internet Filter Review published in http://www.loveismore.es/menu2/estadisticas-pornografia.html emphasizes that the sex industry in the United States during 2006 can be summarized by the following:

  - Video and rental sales: 3.62 billion

  - Internet: 2.84 billion

  - Cable, pay-per-view television, rooms, phone sex: 2.19 billion

  - Exotic dancing clubs: 2 billion

  - Novelties: 1.73 billion

- Magazines: 0.95 billion

- Total: 13.3 billion

On March 2005, the Christianity Today organization published the results of a study called "Christians and Sex" on their Leadership Journal, with the following results:

- 44% church assistants would like to hear more Scripture based teachings about sex.

- 22% of pastors think they should invest more time on this topic.

- 85% of pastors say they speak about sexual topics once a year.

- 57% of pastors say addiction to pornography is the most harmful sexual issue for their congregation.

- 9 out of 10 pastors reported to have given counseling about sexual matters once or more times in a year.

Consequences Produced by the Use of Pornography

- Increase in the number of rapes and sex related crimes.

- Divorces caused by pornographic material brought into the home.

- Pornography leading children into masturbation and experimentation of their sexuality.

- Pornographic images become engraved in the mind forever and cannot be erased, unless we pray for deliverance of that individual, in the name of Jesus.

- Most adults who have used pornography confess, with a great sense of guilt and shame, to be constantly attacked by memories of what they watched.

- Women who allow themselves to be photographed or filmed posing naked for pornographic material come to be dominated by unclean spirits and need to be ministered a deep deliverance.

What is the Solution to be Free from the Use and Consequences of Pornography?

- To repent before God for having used pornography in any way it was.

- To renounce every spirit of pornography, lust, mental fantasies, adultery, fornication, addiction, masturbation; and to command them to leave, in the name of Jesus.

- To pray to the Lord for Him to erase from the mind every single memory of pornography, once and for all.

- To throw away every pornographic material that may be at home, such us videos, magazines, or any object that may lead a person to fall back into the same sin.

6. HOMOSEXUALITY AND LESBIANISM

Homosexuality and lesbianism are the perversion of sexual relations, and they stray from what God established at the beginning of Creation (Genesis 1:27.) The perversion occurs when sexual attraction is felt towards a person of the same sex.

For us to correctly judge all matters relating to homosexuality, we need to go to the Word of God, which gives us the absolute truth about it.

Homosexuality According to the Bible

In the Old Testament, as much as in the New Testament, God forbids homosexuality and lesbianism. Leviticus 18:22 says, *"You shall not lie with a male as with a woman. It is an abomination."* As we can see, from the first days of humanity, God has made His voice heard, but humanity simply covered their ears and ignored His voice.

The New Testament says,

For this reason, God gave them up to vile passions. For even their women exchanged the natural use for what is against nature. Likewise, also the men, leaving the natural use of the woman, burned in their lust for one another, men with men committing what is shameful, and receiving in themselves the penalty of their error which was due. —ROMANS 1:26-27

Clearly, the Bible condemns homosexuality. The problem is that our society, far from using the Bible to establish moral truths, wants to depend on humanistic morals and tends to fall into licentiousness and promiscuity.

Homosexuality is not natural nor does it go with God's plan. It should be enough just to look at men and women's bodies to realize both were designed to complement each other and that they fit together.

However, there is something really important we must understand about God's heart towards homosexuals:

God loves homosexuals, but hates the sin of homosexuality.

Sadly, in the Church of Christ, homosexuals have been judged and criticized. Instead of helping these people and bringing them into the knowledge of truth, we have isolated them from the church. That is why today we must stand firm and establish our position: We are in total disagreement with the sin of homosexuality, because it goes against God's law; but we love the human being who has fallen into this sin, just as Christ loves us. We need to pray for them and want to help them abandon the way of perversion, not shun them.

Causes of Homosexuality

One of the matters we need to understand is that God did not create anybody as a homosexual. The main cause for homosexuality is sin. The Scripture says that in the beginning God made them male and female.

So God created man in His own image; in the image of God He created him; male and female He created them. —GENESIS 1:27

That being said, how then did homosexuality become a factor in the human race? Some of the main causes of homosexuality are:

- **Generational curses**

  These are the consequences to the sin and iniquity of one ancestor that have commuted and manifested themselves upon his descendants, and those consequences replicate from one generation to the other. The cycle of this fatal inheritance can only be interrupted when one descendent with a full conviction of sin, fear of the Lord, and a desire to be free, breaks that chain.

  One way to recognize an ancestor's deviations is when you often hear some people say, "This same thing happened to my father, or in my family." If there is homosexuality in the family, you may hear that type of remark. Well, this is the spirit of homosexuality in action, going from generation to generation through the father or mother's bloodline. It gets transferred by sexual sin in the bloodline, and goes through three, perhaps even four generations.

Homosexuality, as a product of a generational curse, can appear many times due to the practice of anal sex, even if it is practiced within marriage. In this way, children can receive a spirit that will lead them to practice anal sex, whether it be with one gender or the other. Once this practice is initiated (no matter if it is a repeated behavior or a singular event) the door to receive a spirit of homosexuality has been opened.

- **Rejection of the baby's gender**

Sometimes, when a couple is expecting a baby, they desire a girl but receive a boy, or vice versa. Deep in their spirit, those babies receive the message of rejection from their parents. That message is that their sex is not the right one.

As a result of this first rejection from their parents, babies will try and live up to their parent's expectations to try and please them. A parent's rejection of the child's gender is fertile soil for a demonic spirit to come into the life of a baby. In other words, it opens a door for a spirit of homosexuality to manifest in the life of that person.

- **Rebellion against parents**

There are families in which the child is excessively loved due to his or her gender. For example, they put too much emphasis on the fact that he is loved because he is a boy, rather than his being appreciated for his other characteristics. Due to this situation, many sons rebel against their parents, even if it is only to contradict them, and to take off the pressure of being male. They want to remove the "macho" label imposed on them. One way to show their rebellion and to punish their parents is through homosexual behavior. That is why they feel attracted to people of the same sex.

- **Sexual abuse**

This is perhaps the most common cause of homosexual demonization. It originates when a person is sexually abused. It often occurs when one child abuses another; especially if one of them has a generational spirit of homosexuality. In most cases, one of the kids pushes the other, or others, to have a homosexual encounter.

- **Paternal or maternal domination**

Sometimes, when a man is dominated or controlled by his mother, he will face big problems when trying to get married. The mother will assume a position of rejection, seeing his girlfriend as her rival; someone who is trying to steal her son's affection from her. We have seen that in many of these cases, this motivates a man to look to another man to satisfy his sexual desires. The same thing happens with women dominated and controlled by their fathers.

- **Willful homosexual relations**

These relations occur with people that have no generational backgrounds of homosexuality or have never had other connections to homosexuality before in their lives. They are people who simply want to experiment and try it all. When this practice is started in a willful way, doors become wide open for an unclean spirit of homosexuality to enter their lives. Once it does, it is very difficult to get out of homosexuality, unless you receive an intervention of the supernatural power of God.

May we conclude that homosexuality and lesbianism are produced by demons? The answer is, yes, we may.

Demons will use any route to enter the life of a person and distort their sexuality. Once the demons enter that individual by the practice of continuous sin, the demons will control and dominate him or her to the point of enslaving them and, ultimately, killing them.

As we have already seen, the most common doors through which demons enter are: generational curses, rejection of gender by parents, rebellion against parents, sexual abuse, paternal or maternal domination, willful homosexual relations, or any other door, however slightly open it may be.

Testimony: I grew up without my father because he left our home when I was five years old. I was raised among many women and my mother overprotected me since I was little. At school, they would call me girl names. At the age of 14, I started to believe it and began to feel attracted to men. When this began, I felt really bad and started to fight against it. In my desire to change, I started going to church. But at the age of 18, I got tired and said that this was the way I was and there was no solution. Then, I began to go to night clubs and lead my life that way. When my mother found out about it, she began to pray every night –even when I told her I was not going to change.

One night I got home drunk. In my boredom, I turned on the television and while flipping through channels I found TBN. It was there that I heard the preaching that changed my life. That same night, the Lord spoke to my heart and I surrendered to Him. I realized that I was feeling insecure and rejected, I had too much rancor against my father. That night I decided to forgive my father and now I am free. The Lord told me that I am a man. I feel that I have a future, a purpose, and that I am free!

Testimony: Since I was 17 and up to age 24, I practiced lesbianism. I lived with a woman until a female pastor preached the gospel to me. Since then, the Lord delivered me from masculinity. I would cry in my bed and say, "Lord, you are truly faithful and the work that you begin you finish." Now, I desire to have a husband and a family. It is awesome how the Lord transforms us from the inside out! My family is in shock because I no longer dress like a man like I used to. God changed my life!

Testimony: I am not ashamed to tell my testimony because, for the glory of the Lord, He set me free from homosexuality. Everything started when my father rejected me and used to say ugly and offensive words to me, because I used to play with my sister. We were innocent and did not see anything wrong in playing "girl's games." At school, I was also rejected; I had no friends, and they would tell me the same thing my father did. As a result, I was always alone. When at home, I would not say how I felt, and that got rooted inside me and produced a great deal of insecurity in me.

At the age of 18, I came to the United States and began to attend places where homosexuals meet, and got involved in that world. One day, my aunt took me to a Christian church. As soon as I entered that place, I felt like crying so much because the day before I had been at a disco drinking and hanging out with homosexuals. I was so ashamed, but did not cry because I was taught that men are not supposed to cry. Even though that day I did not go to the altar; I managed to receive the conviction that what I was doing was not right. For a while, I continued doing the same thing until I went to a youth retreat. There, the Lord set me free from homosexuality and masturbation. My mom used to cry a lot because of the life I was living. But one day she threw herself to the floor and asked the Lord to have mercy on me and set me free. He answered her clamor.

Today I live happy and I love Christ more than ever before. He spoke to me and said, "I pulled you out of those gay places, from homosexuality, and brought you here." Today I give God all the glory and I love Him with all my heart. I want to tell people who believe that they are born homosexual that that is lie from the Devil. Now I want God to use me to help deliver others.

How to be Free from Homosexuality and Lesbianism

For someone to be free from the spirit of homosexuality, that person needs to have the conviction that it is a sin and goes against nature; that God created men and women to be together and multiply themselves; that the woman is a helper to the man she marries and the husband is the head of the wife, and that cannot be altered.

The following are some steps to reach deliverance from that demonic spirit.

- To repent and confess sin before God.

- To renounce the generational curse of homosexuality that comes through the blood line. To break every curse and cast out every spirit behind that curse.

- To renounce every spirit of homosexuality, rejection, abuse, lust, and sexual perversion.

- To ask the Lord to fill with his presence, every spiritual and emotional void that is left empty when the demonic spirits are removed by Him.

- To stay away from people and places that lead into temptation or back into the same sin.

- To look for deliverance and counseling at a church that knows and understands demonic deliverance.

7. BESTIALITY

The term "bestiality" refers to a beast. The Merriam-Webster Dictionary defines a beast as a four-footed mammal as distinguished from a human being. It is an animal used for loading, especially for domestic use. Bestiality is the sexual relation of humans with animals. The person who practices this has his or her mind full of uncleanness and perversion; and needs deliverance of the soul. Let us read what the Word says about it.

Whoever lies with an animal shall surely be put to death.
—Exodus 22:19

If a woman approaches any animal and mates with it, you shall kill the woman and the animal. They shall surely be put to death. Their blood is upon them. —Leviticus 20:16

I frequently find people, men and women, who have confessed to have had sexual fantasies involving animals. In some cases, this happens because their parents have practiced acts of bestiality. In other cases, their parents have never given them love, and caused them to fall into this sin. I have gotten to know about cases of people who have had sexual relations with dogs, horses, cows, and other animals. Fortunately, the Lord has set them completely free from those unclean spirits.

How to be Free from a Spirit of Bestiality?

- The first thing to do is to repent for having committed the sexual sin of bestiality.

- Then the person must renounce every spirit of bestiality and any related spirit. He or she must command those spirits to leave their life, in the name of Jesus.

8. ABORTIONS

Abortion is the act of murder, the taking of the life of an unborn child that is inside the womb of his or her mother. Women who have practiced abortions must be delivered from a spirit of murder. Sadly, many doctors claim that fetuses that are removed from the womb to end their lives were not yet developed enough to be considered to be alive in the first place, and therefore, nobody is actually dying because of an abortion.

Abortion is the forced removal of a live fetus from the womb of their mother.

What does the Word of God say about abortion? It says that because God has breathed life into them, those fetuses are in fact human beings who are able to feel pain, rejection, love, and hate. They are beings from whom God's gift is being taken away –the gift of the breath of life. When women who have had abortions in their youth get married, sometimes they find it very difficult to get pregnant. This is because they have been sterilized.

There is perhaps no other topic that builds such amount of erroneous information, or half-truths, as the abortion topic. Many times, true facts are ignored or bypassed by those who can do something about it. A great deal of clarifying information about abortion receives little to no attention in public debates because they reveal things that society prefers not to look at.

Next, we will present some data and statistics that reveal the magnitude this malpractice has reached. Much like pornography, this practice has become a multimillionaire business:

- Every year 1,600,000 abortions are performed in the US [1].

- 7% (122,000) are due to the dangers to the mother's physical and psychological health.

- In 1% of the cases there has been a rape or incest.

- 92% (approximately 470,000 abortions) are allegedly made for social, financial, or personal reasons.

- Three out of four women having abortions affirm that a child would interfere with their work, their studies, or other responsibilities [2].

- The number of abortions in the United States is more than a third of the total number of births [3].

- Nearly a fourth of all pregnancies end up in induced abortions [4].

- The United States surpasses all western nations in the number of abortions per every 1,000 women of fertile age [5].

- Young adolescents between the ages of 11 and 19 are responsible for 26% of all abortions in the country.

- Young people between the ages of 18 and 19 have a higher percentage of abortions: 63 per 1,000 [6].

- 45% of minors who practice abortions do it without their parents' consent [7].

Consequences of abortion

The main consequences that people who have had an abortion are:

- Guilt, and

- Remorse

On one occasion, I had before me a woman who underwent more than 15 abortions. She was full of guilt and remorse for having committed so many murders. When we prayed and ministered deliverance over her, the spirits of guilt, remorse, death, and murder came out of her life, and immediately, she began to experience a radical change.

How to be Free from Guilt and Remorse

- Repenting before the Lord and asking Him to forgive the murder committed against a little one in the womb.

- Renouncing the spirit of murder, guilt, remorse, and infertility.

- Asking the Lord to heal the soul of the person that committed the abortion, and also to cleanse her own body.

9. ANAL SEX

Anal sex is a sexual act "against nature" because it goes against the nature established by God. Many times, anal sex is practiced under the pretext of avoiding the risk of pregnancy.

This practice can lead people to fall into other immoral acts such as homosexuality and bestiality. Some women feel so disgusted with this practice that they don't even dare talk about it during a meeting, counseling session, or deliverance.

People who practice or have practiced anal sex need to go under a personal deliverance to be free from spirits of lust, homosexuality, degradation, depravation, perversion, guilt, shame, and low self-esteem.

10. SEXUAL ACTIVITIES WITH DEMONS

This practice comes from many centuries ago. Let us see what the Scripture says about this.

There were giants on the earth in those days, and also afterward, when the sons of God came in to the daughters of men and they bore children to them. Those were the mighty men who were of old, men of renown. —GENESIS 6:4

Throughout History there has been frequent cases of demons approaching women or men to have sexual intercourse with them.

There are two spirits involved in these types of practices:

- The spirit "incubus," who is a demon that looks like a man and stimulates and leads women to sexual pleasure.

- The spirit "succubus", who is a woman like spirit that stimulates and leads men to ejaculation.

Over the last years, many people have been delivered from these spirits. God has given us the great opportunity to be used to deliver them in the powerful name of Jesus of Nazareth.

How to be Free from those Spirits

- Repent before God for opening doors to the enemy.

- Renounce wholeheartedly and repeat this prayer:

"Lord Jesus, in Your name, I renounce every spirit of incubus and succubus, and command them to leave my life by the power of Your precious blood that sets me free."

SYNOPSIS

- Adultery and fornication can be committed with the eyes, heart, mind, and body.

- Lust is to reach the maximum point of indecency and no longer have any restraint in our behavior.

- The three main causes for sexual sins are: generational curses, sexual abuses of the past, and pornography.

- The best thing to do to prevent sexual sins is to flee immediately, and only to flee.

- Masturbation is a sin.

- Adultery and fornication bring about great consequences: the corruption of the soul which causes shame, inner wounds, and death. Those who practice any of these will not inherit the kingdom of God.

- Pornography, in any of its forms, leads people into prostitution and moral depravation. God loves homosexuals, but hates the sin they practice.

- God did not create anyone to be homosexual, but as "male and female He created them."

- Generational curses and sexual abuse are two of the main causes of homosexuality.

- God has the power to set homosexual people free.

- The act of abortion is murder before the eyes of God.

- The person who practices abortion brings guilt and remorse into her life.

STATISTICS

1. Rachel Benson Gold, Abortion and Women's Health, New Cork and Washington DC: The Alan Guttmacher Institute, 1990, pg. 11; Ibid., pg. 20.

2. Ibid., p. 19.

3. The US Disease Control Center reported in the year 1987, 356 abortions per every 1,000 births a year in average. Abortion Surveillance Summaries, June 1990, pg. 23, latest data available.

4. Gold, pg. 11, reports a total of 6,355,000 pregnancies and 1,600,000 abortions.

5. Christopher Tietze and Stanley K. Henshaw, Induced Abortion: A World Review, 6th ed. (New York: Alan Guttmacher Institute, 1986).

6. Stanley K. Henshaw and Jennifer Van Vort, Teenage Abortion, Birth and Pregnancy Statistics: An Update, Family Planning Perspectives, Vol. 20, Num. 4, March/April 1989, the Alan Guttmacher Institute, pg. 85, 86.

7. Alan Guttmacher Institute, Facts in Brief (1989).

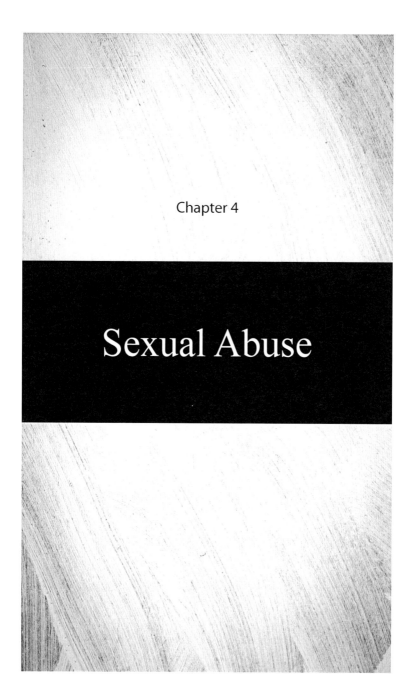

Chapter 4

Sexual Abuse

*S*exual abuse is defined as any sexual activity between two or more individuals without the consent of one of them. It involves any kind of sexual contact done by force or intimidation. It can be between two or more adults, an adult and a minor (this is known as child sexual abuse) or even among minors[1], which is becoming more frequent every day.

Abuse can be manifested in various ways or behaviors, and may go from obscene touching to penetration or having sex with someone against their will.

Sexual abuse is every act of aggression against the genital organs, sexual life, or the reproductive ability of a person.

Generally, the abuser follows a sequence of abusive behaviors that includes many of the following:

- Forces the victim to have sexual intercourse.
- Forces the victim to have sexual intercourse with other people.
- Forces the victim to get naked.

---

1. S. L. Hamby, D. Finkelhor (2000): The victimization of children: recommendations for assessment and instrument development, en J Am Acad Child Adolesc Psychiatry, 39 (7), págs. 29-40.

- Touches the victim's sexual areas or other parts of their body against their will.

- Performs actions that cause pain or humiliate the victim during the sexual intercourse.

- Masturbates himself in front of the victim or forces them to do so.

- Forces the victim to have oral or anal sex.

- Talks to the victim obscenely and/or calls her or him sexual nicknames.

- Forces the victim to have sex with animals.

- May include sexual rituals.

- Forces the victim to use contraceptives or not.

- Forces the victim to have children or to abort them.

- Speaks about his sexual adventures with other women or men.

- Mocks his victim's body, fears, or sexual reactions.

An abuser is more likely to have been a victim of abuse in the past. Once a person has been abused, a door is open for the enemy to enter his or her life immediately. When the victim, be it a boy or a girl, grows up, they begin to experience the same perverted sexual desires as they were exposed to. One way or another, they also become abusers. In all my years of experience, every time I have ministered to a sexual abuser, I have discovered the same pattern: they have first been victims of the same abuse themselves

Sexual abuse is an expression of rejection. Through this act, the abuser expresses his rejection against his victim, innocence, childhood, the entire human race, and against his own abuser.

Even when the most common sexual abuse is the one committed by a man against a woman or a girl, we cannot ignore the fact that there are also women who sexually abuse young boys and men, although it is a lot less frequent.

Let us see some statistics that reveal the magnitude of this immoral behavior.

Statistics

Statistics reveal that in the United States:

- Every minute 1.3 women are raped. This means that 74 women are sexually attacked every hour.

- One out of three women have been sexually molested. 61% of cases are women under 18 years of age.

- One out four women are raped.

- 78% of women knew their rapist.

- Only 16% of rapes get reported to the police.

- 10% of women are abused by their husbands or ex-husbands.

- 11% are abused by their fathers or stepfathers.

- 10% are abused by their boyfriends or ex-boyfriends.

- 16% are abused by other relatives.

- 29% are abused by friends, neighbors, or acquaintances.

Consequences of Sexual Abuse

Victims of sexual abuse are more likely to,

- get confused about their identity, their sexuality, their bodies, and even their emotions,

- return to the experiences that the abused endured in their childhood, as well as the emotional or physical behaviors,

- suppress their memories; many refuse to remember or to admit something happened to them when it is undeniable that it did,

- their lives are filled with fantasies; they live in a world of unreal memories, with imaginary or invisible friends or enemies,

- they are mistrustful; they do not have the ability to trust people, even those one should trust,

- they generally reject others although they have a fear of rejection; which leads them to reject themselves,

- they present a rebellious behavior, and refuse to be under submission or to collaborate,

- they get full of emotional rage due to the abuse,

- they adopt a secretive life style,

- they lose interest in their own physical appearance; often abused people prefer to look unattractive so as not to attract any further abuse to their lives,

- they suffer from eating disorders such as anorexia and bulimia, to escape reality,

- they feel guilty,

- they are unable to respond to love; in many cases, this is not apparent until the person gets married. Many times, marriages break up due to emotional or sexual frigidity on the part of the person who has suffered sexual abuse,

- they fall into promiscuity; some who have been abused suffer premature sexual development and become promiscuous at a very early age,

- they have no desire to live and feel like they want to die,

- they suffer from physical diseases; sometimes, abused people develop a psychosomatic brought on by their subconscious, from which they suffer for a long time so they can hide the real problem,

- their spirit is hurt; they have an inner rage that turns them against God and makes it impossible to have a relationship with Him,

- they unintentionally establish an emotional tie with the abuser.

When this happens, many doors are open to demons, and so they begin a sustained attack. One of the most common strategies is to torment that person with memories of the horror they went through. They recreate inside the victim's mind the most terrorizing moments, with all kinds of details, pushing him or her to display irrational behaviors.

One of the purposes of this chapter is so that you and I, as parents, may become aware of the dangers that may affect our children. After reading this, we cannot just sit back and do nothing. We need to be on alert and be cautious about the people, even other children, around our children. We must know very well the people we trust with the care of our children, and not leave them just anywhere or with just anyone. Let us be certain of that person's psychological and emotional integrity before entrusting our children to them. The enemy is looking for the opportunity to harm your child. We as parents must be clever and always vigilant.

Solutions for Those Who have been Sexually Abused

1. Jesus is the only answer to their pain. The Bible tells us,

    He who sins is of the devil, for the devil has sinned from the beginning. For this purpose, the Son of God was manifested, that He might destroy the works of the devil. —1 JOHN 3:8

    The Spirit of the Lord is upon Me, because He has anointed Me to preach the gospel to the poor; He has sent Me to heal the brokenhearted, to proclaim liberty to the captives and recovery of sight to the blind, to set at liberty those who are oppressed. —LUKE 4:18

2. Repent and ask the Lord to forgive you and those you consider responsible for your abuse, (especially if you have ever blamed Him for having allowed you to be abused, or for not stopping it.

3. Forgive the abuser with all your heart.

    For if you forgive men their trespasses, your heavenly Father will also forgive you. But if you do not forgive men their trespasses, neither will your Father forgive your trespasses. —MATTHEW 6:14-15

4. Renounce the spirits of sexual abuse, rejection, fear of rejection, self-rejection, guilt, lust, fear, insecurity, escapism, rebellion, confusion, frigidity, rage, promiscuity, hurt spirit, and then cast them out! Command them to leave your body, in the name of Jesus.

5. Renounce every physical, emotional, and spiritual tie to your abuser.

6. Ask the Holy Spirit to heal your soul, your spirit, and your body.

7. Declare yourself free in the name of Jesus, right now!

Prayer or Renunciation

Pray the following prayer:

Heavenly Father, now I come before Your presence. First, I repent wholeheartedly for harboring lack of forgiveness, bitterness and hate against those who sexually abused me. In this very moment, I renounce to every spirit of hate, bitterness, and resentment. Right now, willfully, I forgive those people who sexually abused me (if you know them, say their names one by one).

I forgive _____ with all my heart for having abused me. (Do the same with every person and every name you remember).

Lord, right now, I bless them and forgive them. I willfully renounce to every spirit of the enemy who has wanted to come and influence my life when I was abused. I renounce every generational curse in my blood line. I break the spirit of guilt, rejection, lust, escapism, confusion, frigidity, fear, and every spirit attached to sexual abuse, and I cast them out of my life in the name of Jesus. Today I declare myself free! Amen!

Now, ask the Holy Spirit to fill you with His presence.

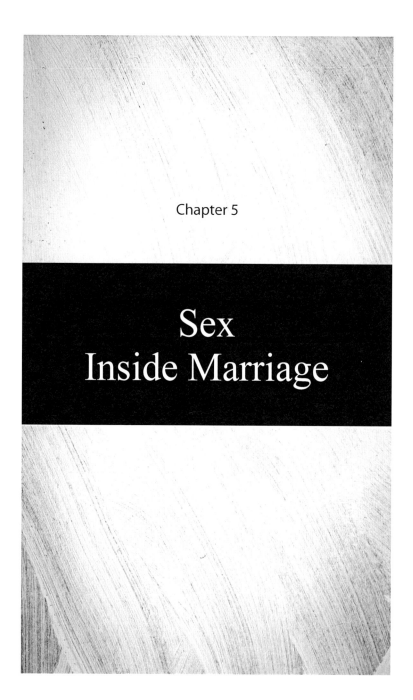

Chapter 5

Sex
Inside Marriage

As we have already established, the creator of sex is God, therefore sex is good and has a good purpose. However, there are people who have a wrong concept about sex, and instead consider it bad and dirty. This deviation of its original concept comes as a consequence of the bad advertising the enemy of humanity has made of it. He has done everything with the intent to destroy marriages and families.

Now Adam knew Eve his wife, and she conceived and bore Cain, and said, "I have acquired a man from the Lord." —GENESIS 4:1

This verse shows us how Adam met his wife intimately. From the beginning of Creation, the Lord's plan was to give us sex to consummate the union of soul and spirit (of man and woman,) through a physical act. This is also the way to fulfill God's commandment in Genesis 1:28, when God says to Adam and Eve, *"be fruitful and multiply."* But in Genesis 9:1 the same words appear. There, God blesses Noah and his children, saying, *"Be fruitful and multiply; fill the earth and subdue it."*

Sex is a blessing that leads us to fulfill God's plans.

Parameters of the Sex Established by God

The enemy has taken on the task of disguising lies as truths and confusing humanity, bringing about "modern" ideas about sex. One of the strongest and repeated excuses for sex outside God's order is, "if there is love you can have sex, even outside of marriage."

The Bible, however, teaches us that love is not a guideline that allows people to have sex, and that it is within God's parameter. The only valid parameter set forth by God for sex is within the covenant of marriage, and is the only one He blesses. The fact that a man and woman love each other does not means is right to have sexual intercourse while single; every sexual relation outside marriage is sin.

God created sex to be enjoyed inside marriage, between a man and a woman.

Purpose by Which God Created Sex

But did He not make them one, having a remnant of the Spirit? And why one? He seeks godly offspring. Therefore, take heed to your spirit, and let none deal treacherously with the wife of his youth. —MALACHI 2:15

- **God created sex to procreate and have descendants for Himself.**

  And God blessed them, saying, "Be fruitful and multiply, and fill the waters in the seas, and let birds multiply on the earth." —GENESIS 1:22

  In the beginning of Creation, God commanded men to be fruitful and multiply. Likewise, He blessed the woman's womb to bear his seed and procreate to increase and multiply the offspring of God.

- **God created sex to give man and woman pleasure.**

  Let your fountain be blessed, and rejoice with the wife of your youth. As a loving deer and a graceful doe, let her breasts satisfy you at all times; and always be enraptured with her love. —PROVERBS 5:18-19

  God placed the sexual impulses inside men and women, not to torture them but to allow them to feel joy and plenitude; and that way, they would be able to rejoice together their whole life.

Sex is not dirty, sex is not bad; even though that is the idea the Devil has sold us for centuries.

Truly, the enemy has used sex to destroy entire families, through abuses, infidelities, frigidity, impotence, and others. But that does not mean sex is bad or dirty, because if practiced inside marriage, between a man and a woman, sex is beautiful; as everything that has been created by God.

The enemy has robbed many women of the ability to enjoy sex in their marriages, making them believe sex is dirty. Those lies may have entered their minds as a consequence of childhood or adolescent sexual traumas which has caused them to neglect sex and see it as something negative in their lives. Those women need inner healing; they need to know God's truth about sex and themselves. Many of them have lost, or are losing their marriages because of those traumas that have caused them to become frigid during the sexual act. In response, their husbands, unable to change the situation, end up abandoning them.

Both, husband and wife have sexual needs and instincts that must be satisfied within marriage. That need cannot be ignored because sooner or later, they will suffer grave consequences in their relationship.

Is it Right to Deny Sexual Relations to your Spouse?

There is a Biblical truth we all need to know. When a person gets married, meaning that he or she gets joined to another in marriage, his or her body no longer belongs to them; but, on the contrary, the Bible says that the spouse is now the owner of their body.

No *man nor woman can say no to sexual intercourse with their spouse, unless it be to seek God's face in prayer.*

Let the husband render to his wife the affection due her, and likewise also the wife to her husband. The wife does not have authority over her own body, but the husband does. And likewise, the husband does not have authority over his own body, but the wife does. Do not deprive one another except with consent for a time, that you may give yourselves to fasting and prayer; and come together again so that Satan does not tempt you because of your lack of self-control.
—1 CORINTHIANS 7:3-5

Conjugal duty consists of agreeing to have sex with the spouse. It is interesting to note that the Bible calls it a "duty." It does not say, "if you feel like it…" Inside marriage, none of the spouses is the owner of their own body, that body now belongs to the spouse.

The Amplified Bible says,

The husband should give to his wife her conjugal rights (goodwill, kindness, and what is due her as his wife), and likewise the wife to her husband. For the wife does not have [exclusive] authority and control over her own body, but the husband [has his rights]; likewise, also the husband does not have [exclusive] authority and control over his body, but the wife [has her rights]. Do not refuse and deprive and defraud each other [of your due marital rights], except perhaps by mutual consent for a time, so that you may devote yourselves unhindered to prayer. But afterwards resume marital relations, lest Satan tempt you [to sin] through your lack of restraint of sexual desire. —1 Corinthians 7:3-5*

The Only Period of Abstinence Allowed

The only period in which the couple can abstain from sex is when, in common agreement, both give themselves to **prayer and fast;** with the condition of coming back together as one once that period of abstinence is ended.

Why should couples not deny one another in their conjugal duties? Because if they do so, the enemy will take advantage and it will be easier to tempt them to sin against God, looking outside what they do not find at home. The Scripture recommends this, *"…so that Satan does not tempt you because of your lack of self-control"* (1 Corinthians 7:5.)

If there is a woman sexually denying herself to her husband, or vice versa, they should know that with this action they are throwing their spouse in the arms of the enemy; they are pushing them to be an easy prey for temptation. It is important that an immediate change be produced in that situation.

There are women who use many excuses to avoid having sexual relations with their husbands. The most common excuses can be:

89

a headache, tiredness, children, age, cold, heat, the time, and so on. Women, remember that men are more sexually active than you; and denying yourself to fulfill your duty as a wife can lead him to look for an illicit relationship.

THE BIGGEST OBSTACLE IN THE SEXUAL LIFE OF A WOMAN

The biggest obstacle in a woman's sexual life is sexual frigidity. This may come as a consequence of abuses, mainly during childhood.

Sexual Frigidity

Frigidity is the inability to enjoy the sexual act and reach the fulfillment of orgasm. Most women with this kind of trouble cannot experience orgasms; and if they do, they are weak and incomplete.

What is an orgasm? It is the highest point of pleasure in the sexual life of a woman. It is the instant in which she reaches the climax of satisfaction during an intimate relation with her husband.

Although sexual frigidity is the major cause of women being unable to reach an orgasm, this does not take away the responsibility the husband has to help his wife reach it. The husband should use caresses, kisses, and words of love to help her. He has to understand that the woman is different from him, and he must be patient and wait longer to help her to achieve climax.

Sexual frigidity in a woman is as destructive as is lust in a man.

Sometimes, these enemies (frigidity and lust) operate together under one roof. Consequently, families are destroyed.

If sexual desires are not satisfied inside marriage they can lead to seeking illicit relationships or destructive behaviors, such as adultery, pornography, masturbation, and so forth.

Testimony: Some time ago, a father was put in jail because he had sexually abused his own daughter. When he was ministered in deliverance, he admitted his sin. One of the reasons that led him to do so was because his wife had denied him sexual relations for an extended period of time. After that, he began to look at his daughter with lust. Even though this is not an excuse at all for any abuse, we can see how this fact opened a door to the enemy to enter and destroy a family. For this reason, it is important for the couple to be well-informed and in good communication about the dangers that can be brought about when one spouse denies sexual intercourse to the other. With this knowledge, the problem can be corrected and the enemy can't take advantage of their ignorance. Remember that understanding each other is very important in these cases.

Causes for Sexual Frigidity

Recent investigations show that there is no specific cause for frigidity. However, the main detonators that may be setting off this problem may be of spiritual, emotional, or physical origin. Let us study the most common causes of frigidity.

1. **Sexual abuse from the past.** This cause can be catastrophic in the life of a person, so much so that it may even lead to death. Sometimes, frigidity can be apparent as early as childhood, as a result of incest, rape, or a member of the family having sexually molested a girl.

When a person has been sexually abused, different areas of their life are affected, and the consequences are many. For example: resentment, revenge, guilt, lack of forgiveness, bitterness, fear of men, or fear of sexual intercourse. All these traumas and memories of the past may cause a woman to be unable to fully enjoy the sexual act in their marriage. Instead they feel guilty and see sex as a dirty, painful, traumatic, and despicable thing. It is an act in which she does not want to participate, and if she does, she will be defensive and full of fear.

Sexual frigidity caused by past sexual abuse may lead to the destruction of a family; and the woman who endures it has no opportunity to live a normal life, unless the love and supernatural power of Jesus Christ intervenes. The Lord is the only one who can heal, set free, and restore a woman in this state. The will of God is that every woman may be able to enjoy sexual intercourse with her husband, and that she may reach orgasm every time she and her husband join together in the act of love.

2. **Physical and emotional fatigue, or being overweight.** Every normal body's functions are weakened when a person is fatigued or preoccupied. An emotionally or physically tired woman will not be a loving wife. Then there are other women who are upset about being overweight, and their appearance, and the rolls of fat on their bodies, often overreacting to them. They experience a sense of low self-esteem and feel that they are no longer attractive in their husband's eyes. The solution to both these problems is very simple; the tired wife should take time for herself, to rest and enjoy a vacation. The overweight wife should start a diet and a daily exercise program, and she will soon see the results that.

3. **Weak vaginal musculature.** This problem happens to most women after they have given birth. The vagina is left excessively relaxed and the adjacent muscles that kept it firm and sensitive begin to sag. The same problem occurs when women reach middle age.

Approximately two thirds of women not reaching orgasm during intercourse with their husbands suffer from this serious problem; but the solution is at hand. There are certain techniques and exercises physicians recommend which may remedy the problem in the short time with no complications at all.

OBSTACLES IN A MAN'S SEXUAL LIFE

Sexual Impotency

Until some years ago, sexual impotency was a repeated incapacity to perform or sustain an erection firm enough to have satisfactory sexual intercourse. Now, this problem is medically called "erectile dysfunction." At the same time, sexual impotency has become a broader term that includes other issues affecting sexual intercourse and reproduction, such us ejaculation problems.

Until today, medicine has not been able to prevent sexual impotency in men. It has only developed some drugs to help initiate an erection. Not a day goes by without a man going to a doctor to seek consultation about these kinds of troubles, or to be prescribed this popular drug that initiates an erection. However, there are many men who don't realize the real problem that is affecting them until they reach a certain age and the illness is at a very advanced stage. So, it is extremely important for you to know your body and how it reacts.

Sexual instinct in men manifests since childhood, but reaches its peak between 18 and 22 years old. After that age, it begins to decline slowly; at such a slow speed that most men don't realize it until they are more than 30 years old, or even in their late forties. And many will not detect it until they are around sixty years old.

The first time a man realizes he cannot ejaculate anymore, it is like a tragedy for him. After forty years of age, a man's sexual organ is his brain.

Your sexual performance will be as good as the idea you have of yourself.

If you consider yourself strong and effective, that is the way you will be; similarly, if you think of yourself as the contrary, so you will be. Every man must know his body and the fact that, for example, he can ejaculate two to five times a day (depending on his age and physical health.)

What is ejaculation? It is the moment in which the man reaches his sexual climax during his intimate relations with a woman. Ejaculation is the fast and violent release of semen (a milky liquid) from a man's penis. Each drop of semen transports around 300 million spermatozoids for the purpose of fertilizing the woman's ovule, to multiply the species. Knowing what ejaculation is can help us analyze another big obstacle in a man's sexual life.

Premature ejaculation

Premature ejaculation is a disorder of sexual potency characterized by the early emission of semen when introducing the penis into the vagina, or immediately before or after. It is the inability to hold the emission of semen during the time it takes to bring the wife to her own climax.

It is hard to believe that this inconvenience affects more young men than older ones. Statistics show that young men are the majority when it comes to consuming drugs to help them perform consistent sexual intercourse. As a sad consequence, they feel deficient, frustrated, sick, and incomplete, and thus their wives feel unsatisfied.

Main Causes for Sexual Impotency

The main causes for sexual impotency are similar to the causes for women's frigidity in the sense that they may be of spiritual, emotional, or of physical origin. Let us study some of them.

1. **The influence of a spirit of sickness.** This may be the product of a generational curse. Sometimes, a bad spirit provokes physical illnesses which bring consequences of impotency and even infertility.

2. **A spirit of fear.** When a man realizes his sexual impotency, his inner being becomes filled with all kinds of fears. For example: fear of a wife's rejection, fear to being unable to satisfy her, fear of being compared to another man, fear of losing the ability to get an erection, fear to not being able to ejaculate, etc. All of this attracts another bad spirit into his life; and that is the spirit of guilt.

3. **Lack of forgiveness and bitterness.** Many men become impotent due to the big troubles they carry inside their hearts, such as lack of forgiveness, bitterness, and hate. When they begin to forgive those who hurt, abused, and offended them, this sexual dysfunction also disappears and their sexual lives improve substantially.

4. **A poor physical condition and obesity.** It is important for each man to develop habits of physical exercise and eating a healthy diet. It is proven that when the man achieves a good physical condition and sustains a healthy weight, his self-esteem rises. This leads him to become more sexually active.

We may mention even more causes for sexual impotency; for example, mental problems, depression, sense of guilt, addiction to smoking, drugs, medications, alcoholic beverages, and the frequent practice of masturbation.

Nonetheless, the most recent investigations show that sexual impotency is on the rise at an extremely fast paced. For this reason, it is important for men to know how to deal with it.

Some Advice for Men to Enjoy Sexual Intercourse with their own Wives

- Know your body.

- Seek first your wife's satisfaction, and then your own.

- Remember, the woman must be stimulated with caresses, soft words, and tender touching. You may be in a rush, but she is not.

- Love your wife as the person she is; she is not an object. A man may gain his wife's affection when he loves and treats her as a valued being in his life.

- Prepare a loving atmosphere with your wife at the beginning of the day so she can respond positively at night.

- Choose the words that heal your wife's heart. Make her feel appreciated, beautiful; let her know you find her attractive and that you need her.

- Keep an open line of communication at all times.

When a man does these things, then the woman will respond positively to sexual intercourse and find pleasure in it.

Some Advice for Women to Enjoy Sexual Intercourse with their own Husbands

- Keep the correct attitude towards sex and know your share of responsibility in the marriage's conjugal duties.

- It is important that women have a healthy mentality, specifically on these three areas:

  - What she thinks about sex;

  - What she thinks of herself; and

  - What she thinks of her husband.

When a woman has a healthy mentality in these three areas, she becomes able to enjoy sex within her marriage.

- It is important for a woman to take good care of her physical appearance, wearing make-up, practicing good hygiene, taking care of her whole body and always looking feminine.

- The woman must understand that men are visually stimulated, so your appearance is important.

- Do not assume a passive attitude with your husband when it comes to the sexual act, rather respond to him appropriately.

- When you have tried it all, but still do not feel fulfilled during sexual intercourse, ask the grace of the Holy Spirit to help you. He will give you the favor and power to achieve it; because it is the will of God for Christian couples to enjoy sex within marriage.

Questions about Sex within Marriage

1. Is oral and anal sex allowed by God?

No, it is not allowed. It is considered a sexual aberration. God created every organ of the body to fulfill a specific function. The mouth was made to worship Him and to take food in; not to introduce the sexual organ. Besides, doctors have been very clear about this, saying that through this practice many microbes can be introduced via a person's mouth. The Bible does not tell us anything about it, but I have found that people who practice oral sex give way to spirits of lust into their lives.

2. What is menopause and what is its cause?

Menopause is a gradual decreasing of the ovular activity in women.

As a woman advances in age, her estrogen reserve, which is responsible for the production of ovules, begins to decrease; this causes irregularities in her menstruation. This is called the menopause period. As a consequence, they may experience swollen breasts, and weight gain around the stomach. Some women report feeling too much heat, while others suffer from depression or become very irritable. Every woman going through this symptom must go to the doctor; but above all, must pray to the Lord to rejuvenate her, as well as to keep a positive mental attitude.

3. At what age does menopause begin?

For most women, it begins at the age of forty-five, but the ceasing of the menstrual period does not occur until they have reached their mid-fifties.

4. Is sex allowed during menstruation?

Let us see what the Scripture says:

Also you shall not approach a woman to uncover her nakedness as long as she is in her customary impurity.
—Leviticus 18:19

In the Old Testament, God forbade sexual intercourse during the period of menstruation. I believe this was because it is not a hygienic period. Besides, a woman's organs get very delicate during this time. Modern physicians say it does no harm; but I prefer to let myself be guided by the Word of God.

5. Is sex allowed during pregnancy?

Yes, it is. Doctors say it is recommended to have sex up until six weeks prior to giving birth.

6. Is it permissible to use sex as a weapon to manipulate and control the spouse?

No! It is not right, and the Bible forbids it. This can be used by the enemy as a door to enter and bring along a spirit of manipulation and control to attack the lives of people.

7. Can a man commit adultery with his mind and heart?

Yes! For that reason, it is important not to entertain those kinds of thoughts. Adultery may be committed with the eyes, the mind, the heart, and the body.

But I say to you that whoever looks at a woman to lust for her has already committed adultery with her in his heart.
—Matthew 5:28

SYNOPSIS

- God is the creator of sex; thus, sex is something beautiful and was made for us to enjoy it.

- The set Biblical parameter to have sex is within marriage. Love is not reason enough to have sexual intercourse if the couple has not been married yet.

- Men and women must fulfill their conjugal duties, so that Satan will not be able to tempt them with illicit relationships or practices.

- The biggest obstacle that keeps women from enjoying the sexual act is frigidity.

- Sexual frigidity may be caused by abuses from the past, emotional or physical fatigue, or by vaginal muscular weakness.

- Sexual impotency, including premature ejaculation, are the biggest sexual problems men face.

- Sexual impotency may be caused by the influence of a bad spirit, fear, lack of forgiveness, bitterness, bad physical shape, or being insecure from being overweight.

- It is of extreme importance that men and women view sex, themselves, and their spouses in the correct manner, so that they may have a happy sexual life.

Prayer of Renunciation

If you have problems of sexual impotency or frigidity and want to be free, please pray this prayer out loud and in faith,

"Heavenly Father, I repent with all my heart from every lack of forgiveness, bitterness, and resentment I have kept in my heart.

I, voluntarily, forgive all those people who sexually abused or molested me during my childhood or adolescence. Heavenly Father, I ask You to forgive me for having sexually denied myself to my spouse; and right now, I renounce to the spirit of sexual abuse, impotency, fear, guilt, shame, rejection, emotional and sexual frigidity; I break it and cast it out in the name of Jesus. I renounce also to every spirit of masturbation. Now, Heavenly Father, I ask You to heal any physical problem in my body that may be affecting my sexual life, and I declare myself healed and free, in the name of Jesus. Amen!"

Now, breathe deeply and let the Holy Spirit set you free. Be free! Believe it by faith!

If you prayed this prayer out loud, repeat it again and again. Begin to breathe in and out deeply and command every spirit of the enemy to come out of your body.

Friend, reader, at this very moment I will pray for you. I declare you free and healed. I declare that your sexual life changes for good, and that you are transformed completely, in the name of Jesus. Amen!

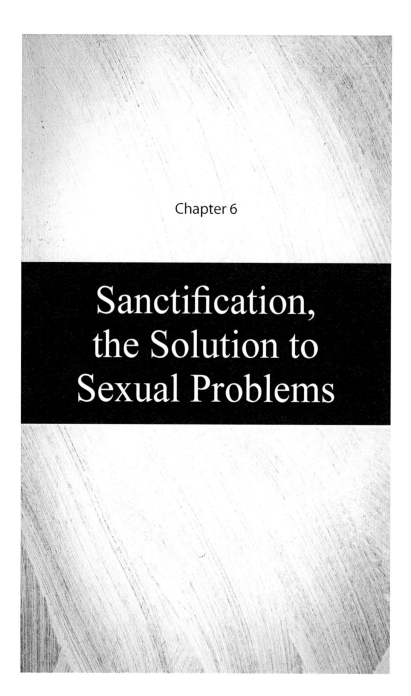

Chapter 6

Sanctification, the Solution to Sexual Problems

The will of God since the beginning of creation has been the sanctification of His children. The Scripture says,

For this is the will of God, your sanctification: that you should abstain from sexual immorality. —1 THESSALONIANS 4:3

As we have been studying, God created sex and made it pure, to fulfill divine purposes. Sadly, the devil has used it to make people sin, and commit aberrations and depravations that destroy the human race. From then on, a great number of sexual sins exist. This chapter will be dedicated to study the God given solution to overcome these kinds of sins: sanctification.

The Meaning of Being Holy

Holy is one who is separated, set apart, and consecrated for God. This does not mean that they are perfect, but it refers to those who have accepted Jesus as the Lord and Savior of their lives. They are people who have decided to walk in His ways, according to His purpose, and fulfill His will.

The will of God is for us to step aside from fornication, adultery, uncleanness, homosexuality, masturbation, and all illicit sexual practices.

HOW TO STAY APART OR BE SET APART FOR GOD

Fleeing sexual sins

Thus he left all that he had in Joseph's hand, and he did not know what he had except for the bread which he ate. Now Joseph was handsome in form and appearance. And it came to pass after these things that his master's wife cast longing eyes on Joseph, and she said, "Lie with me." But he refused and said to his master's wife, "Look, my master does not know what is with me in the house, and he has committed all that he has to my hand. There is no one greater in this house than I, nor has he kept back anything from me but you, because you are his wife. How then can I do this great wickedness, and sin against God?" So it was, as she spoke to Joseph day by day, that he did not heed her, to lie with her or to be with her. But it happened about this time, when Joseph went into the house to do his work, and none of the men of the house was inside, that she caught him by his garment, saying, "Lie with me." But he left his garment in her hand, and fled and ran outside.
—Genesis 39:6-12

Temptation is not to be resisted; it is to be fled from

If you do not flee sexual temptation but instead you entertain it or play with it, it becomes ten times stronger than you. At that instance, your chances to defeat it will be very little. When we read the story about Joseph, we realize that he made the decision to flee and run away from temptation. It was not the other person who made the decision for him. This tells us that if God already established that His will is our sanctification, we must choose to set ourselves apart, to stay apart, and flee from sexual immorality.

What gave Joseph the grace to flee and defeat temptation? The Holy Spirit put fear of God in him and he reflected saying, *"how would I do this great evil, and sin against God?"* On this day, ask the Holy Spirit to put the fear of God on your eyes, your mind, your body, and your heart.

When we make the decision to run away from temptation, the Holy Spirit gives us His grace and His strength to do so.

All of us as believers have a divine grace over our lives. This does not mean we should not be ready to flee temptation. In the New Testament, the Lord also tells us to flee from sexual sins.

Flee sexual immorality. Every sin that a man does is outside the body, but he who commits sexual immorality sins against his own body. —1 CORINTHIANS 6:18

Here, the word "flee" is the translation of the Greek verb pheugo, which means to leave running away in search of security. In a metaphorical sense, it means to escape to avoid something abhorrent, especially the vices. It also means to escape to save oneself or to put oneself out of danger.

We could illustrate this by comparing it to a bomb when it is about to explode and we have to run away desperately to save our lives and avoid getting killed in the explosion. We should react in that same way in the face of sexual temptation because, if we fall in it, we will surely die.

Paul also says this in the same way,

Do not lay hands on anyone hastily, nor share in other people's sins; keep yourself pure. —1 TIMOTHY 5:22

Other people's sins of which the apostle is talking about in this Scripture are very strong: evil desires, sexual immorality, greed, and all kinds of experiences that are against the will of God.

For this is the will of God, your sanctification: that you should abstain from sexual immorality. —1 THESSALONIANS 4:3

Here, God again gives us the responsibility to abstain and be set apart for Him. We make the decision and the Holy Spirit gives us the grace and the strength to do so.

What Happens if We Do Not Set Ourselves Apart from Sexual Immorality?

The anointing and the presence of God will stay away from us. The Bible says,

To keep you from the evil woman, from the flattering tongue of a seductress. Do not lust after her beauty in your heart, nor let her allure you with her eyelids. For by means of a harlot a man is reduced to a crust of bread; and an adulteress will prey upon his precious life. Can a man take fire to his bosom, and his clothes not be burned? Can one walk on hot coals, and his feet not be seared? So is he who goes in to his neighbor's wife; whoever touches her shall not be innocent. People do not despise a thief if he steals to satisfy himself when he is starving. Yet when he is found, he must restore sevenfold; he may have to give up all the substance of his house. Whoever commits adultery with a woman lacks understanding; he who does so destroys his own soul. Wounds and dishonor he will get, and his reproach will not be wiped away. —PROVERBS 6:24-33

The sin of sexual immorality has destroyed great men and women of God, who one day moved under a powerful anointing, and whose hands were used by God to make extraordinary miracles. Also, marriages of many years were destroyed in an instant, flourishing businesses fell, healthy and strong men were infected with HIV and other illnesses in a single moment.

Without exception, every immoral act brings around serious consequences, such as: the destruction of families, and the disobedience and rebellion of children. Those once obedient children end up leaving their homes and living in addictions, full of hatred and rancor, because of their parent's sexual immorality.

Sexual immorality has hurt and killed many sons and daughters of God.

For by means of a harlot a man is reduced to a crust of bread; and an adulteress will prey upon his precious life. —PROVERBS 6:26

Let us see the case of Samson in the Scripture,

So the woman bore a son and called his name Samson; and the child grew, and the Lord blessed him. And the Spirit of the Lord began to move upon him at Mahaneh Dan between Zorah and Eshtaol. —JUDGES 13:24-25

And the Spirit of the Lord came mightily upon him, and he tore the lion apart as one would have torn apart a young goat, though he had nothing in his hand. But he did not tell his father or his mother what he had done. —JUDGES 14:6

When he came to Lehi, the Philistines came shouting against him. Then the Spirit of the Lord came mightily upon him; and the ropes that were on his arms became like flax that is burned with fire, and his bonds broke loose from his hands. He found a fresh jawbone of a donkey, reached out his hand and took it, and killed a thousand men with it. —JUDGES 15:14-15

As we can see in the three biblical texts above, God began to use Samson in a powerful way, until a woman tempted him and he ended up destroyed.

Afterward it happened that he loved a woman in the Valley of Sorek, whose name was Delilah. —JUDGES 16:4

Then she said to him, "How can you say, 'I love you,' when your heart is not with me? You have mocked me these three times, and have not told me where your great strength lies." And it came to pass, when she pestered him daily with her words and pressed him, so that his soul was vexed to death, that he told her all his heart, and said to her, "No razor has ever come upon my head, for I have been a Nazirite to God from my mother's womb. If I am shaven, then my strength will leave me, and I shall become weak, and be like any other man." When Delilah saw that he had told her all his heart, she sent and called for the lords of the Philistines, saying, "Come up once more, for he has told me all his heart." So the lords of the Philistines came up to her and brought the money in their hand. Then she lulled him to sleep on her knees, and called for a man and had him shave off the seven locks of his head. Then she began to torment him, and his strength left him. And she said, "The Philistines are upon you, Samson!" So he awoke from his sleep, and said, "I will go out as before, at other times, and shake myself free!" But he did not know that the Lord had departed from him. —JUDGES 16:15-20

One of God's heroes, a giant of the God Almighty, died among debris and eyeless; he felt hurt and died because of the sin of adultery and fornication. He died young and did not fulfill his purpose on earth. Unlike Joseph, Samson never fled, never ran away or set himself apart, and sin became so strong that it reduced his soul to distress and he ended up dead.

On the contrary, Joseph ran away. It is true he was thrown in jail for doing the right thing. Nevertheless, later on he ended up in the Pharaoh's palace as a prime minister, after everything that had happened.

The only thing God needs to do so that we may have a bad time in everything, is not to cut off our finances, or send us a sickness, or even strike us with lightning, but to take away His anointing and His presence from our lives.

When the presence and anointing of God are not with us, everything we touch becomes sterile, dried up, so then it stops and dies.

We cannot afford to continue to sin. Samson was a greatly anointed man, but without holiness he was nothing. Power without character is dangerous; because the greater the power, the higher the fall. David's case, however, was different because he was powerfully anointed, but whenever he sinned he was quick to ask God for His forgiveness; he would repent and work on living in holiness before the eyes of God.

Levels of Holiness, Sanctification, and Separation to which God is Taking Us

Once we make the decision of setting ourselves apart and realize holiness is the will of God, then He will bring us through a process of sanctification. There are two words to describe this, one in Greek and one in Hebrew, respectively: "nazar" that means to set apart or separate from, and "Kadesh" which means to separate or set apart for.

1. God "underline sets us apart or separates us from" sin.

Jesus overcame at the cross and separated us from the root of sin, and now we have dominion over it. When we are born again, authority is given to us; and sin can no longer take lordship over us.

For sin shall not have dominion over you, for you are not under law but under grace. —ROMANS 6:14

The reason many believers are still struggling with sin is because they have not believed God's promise that tells us we are free from sin.

2. God "underline sets us apart or separates us from" the world.

God in His Word commands us to separate ourselves from the world, because it is not possible to be friends with God and with the world at the same time.

Adulterers and adulteresses! Do you not know that friendship with the world is enmity with God? Whoever therefore wants to be a friend of the world makes himself an enemy of God. —JAMES 4:4

There are certain things of the world to which we are still attached, things that we love and still do. But we must make a decision to separate ourselves from them. For example, the disco, dancing places, vocabulary, drinks, friends, and other things.

3. God "underline sets us apart or separates us from" some good things.

When we do good things but they occupy first place in our lives, or have a greater priority than God, the Lord will take them away for us to be able to set ourselves apart for

Himself. Some of those things may be friendships, sports, hobbies, businesses, and other things.

4. God "<u>separates us or sets us apart for</u>" Himself.

This is the stage in which we chose to serve God with our talents, with our money; we chose to fulfill the purpose of God and do His will, no matter the price we need to pay.

Many men who have fallen in sin had *"separated from"* sin, had *"separated from"* the world, had *"separated from"* the good things, but never "set themselves apart for" God.

To separate or set apart for God involves many things, such as:

- Developing an intimate relationship with God every day, so this will become a continuous, growing, and persistent relationship.

- Establishing a separation through fasting and prayer, and doing this as part of a lifestyle.

- Serving God wholeheartedly and fulfilling His purpose.

- Committing oneself to the Lord in spirit, soul, and body.

- Committing oneself to being true disciples of Jesus and to winning souls for the Kingdom.

- Developing an obsession and passion to preach, teach, and extend the Kingdom of God all around.

God's Promise for those Who Set Themselves Apart *(kadesh)* for Him

Nevertheless the solid foundation of God stands, having this seal: "The Lord knows those who are His," and, "Let everyone who names the name of Christ depart from iniquity." But in a great house there are not only vessels of gold and silver, but also of wood and clay, some for honor and some for dishonor. Therefore if anyone cleanses himself from the latter, he will be a vessel for honor, sanctified and useful for the Master, prepared for every good work. —2 TIMOTHY 2:19-21

God's ultimate goal is to take us to being instruments, useful vessels for His Kingdom and to bring us into complete purity and holiness. God is not who determines what kind of vessel we will be in His hands, be they vessels of silver, wood, clay, or gold. We are the ones who determine what kind of vessels we want to be, by separating ourselves from sexual iniquity and from every sin that is there.

David sinned but repented and humbled himself. That is why God restored Him to be king of Israel. David would live set apart for God and separated in the desert, in His presence. On the other hand, Samson did not show any humbleness, nor did he live in prayer; he did not set himself apart for God.

We are living in a day and age where God is going to judge those believers who have been practicing sin as a lifestyle. The Lord has been waiting for us to separate ourselves from immorality, from the world, and even those things and people that are obstacles in the way to consecrate ourselves to Him. That is why the time is coming when God will have to judge our condition.

Are you willing to separate yourself from sexual immorality? Are you willing to obey God and leave friendships and things of the world that you still love? Are you available to be consecrated, separated, and set apart for God's use only? Are you willing to be an instrument of honor for God? Are you willing to commit yourself to serve God with all your being, no matter the cost?

If your answer is "yes" to all these questions, you are a strong candidate to be called a "friend of God", set apart for His service, ready to be an instrument in His hands; someone that will bring Him glory and will advance His Kingdom all around the earth.

In my case, I have the conviction that I was born to serve God and be set apart for Him for the rest of my life to expand His Kingdom.

SYNOPSIS:

- The will of God is for believers to be sanctified and stay away from sexual immorality.

- We believers are holy because we have been separated and set apart for God.

- The way to separate ourselves from sexual immorality is by fleeing and staying away from it.

- We are the ones to make the decision of fleeing and God gives us His grace to do so.

- If we separate ourselves from sexual immorality, the anointing and the presence of God will never stay away from us.

- Samson was destroyed by sexual sin.

- The four levels of holiness every believer will experience are: separation from sin, from the world, and from the good things that keep him from his purpose; and lastly, he will be set apart for God and will be an instrument of honor in His hands.

- We must judge ourselves, make the decision and have the desire to become useful instruments in God's hands; and be willing to advance His Kingdom on earth.

About the Author

Active in ministry for over twenty years, Apostle Guillermo Maldonado is the founder of King Jesus International Ministry—one of the fastest-growing multicultural churches in the United States—which has been recognized for its development of kingdom leaders and for visible manifestations of God's supernatural power.

Apostle Maldonado earned a master's degree in practical theology from Oral Roberts University and a doctorate in divinity from Vision International University. He is a spiritual father to more than 300 pastors and apostles of local and international churches in 50 countries, which form part of a growing association, the Network of the Supernatural Movement.

Some of his most recent books are: How to Walk in the Supernatural Power of God, The Glory of God, The Kingdom of Power, Supernatural Transformation, Supernatural Deliverance, Daily Encounters with God, and Divine Encounter with the Holy Spirit. In addition, he preaches the message of Jesus Christ and His redemptive power on his national and international television program, The Supernatural Now, which airs on TBN, Daystar, the Church Channel, and fifty other networks, thus with a potential outreach and impact to more than two billion people across the world.

Apostle Maldonado resides in Miami, Florida, with his wife and partner in ministry, Ana, and their two sons, Bryan and Ronald.

BIBLIOGRAFÍA

Biblia Plenitud. 1960 Reina-Valera Revisión, ISBN: 089922279X, Editorial Caribe, Miami, Florida.

Dewberry, Harold R, PhD. *Feed my Sheep, Feed my Lambs*.

Dewberry, Harold R, PhD. New Vine Press, PO Box 17, Chichester West Sussex, PO 20 6YB, England, Copyright 1993, ISBN: 1874367396, Third edition 1995.

Diccionario Español a Inglés, Inglés a Español. Editorial Larousse S.A., impreso en Dinamarca, Núm. 81, México, ISBN: 2034202007, ISBN: 70607371X, 1993.

El Pequeño Larousse Ilustrado. 2002 Spes Editorial, S.L. Barcelona; Ediciones Larousse, S.A. de C.V. México, D.F., ISBN: 970-22-0020-2.

Expanded Edition the Amplified Bible. Zondervan Bible Publishers. ISBN: 0310951682, 1987 – Lockman Foundation, USA.

Gibson, Noel y Phyl. *Evicting Demonic Intrudors*. New Vine Press, PO Box 17, Chichester West Sussex, PO 20 6YB, England, Copyright 1993, ISBN: 1874367094

Hewett, James S. *Illustrations Unlimited*. Tyndale House Publishers, Inc., Wheaton, Illinois, 1988.

Hobson, Peter. *Sex and Morality and Demons*, 1ra edición, impreso en Srilanka por New Life Literature, LTD Kata Nunayake, 1996, p. 85. ISBN: 0947252088.

Horrobin, Peter J. *Healing Throught Deliverance*, The Biblical Basis (volume 1), edition 1991, 1994.

Horrobin, Peter J. *Healing Throught Deliverance*, The Practical Ministry (volume 2), 1995 first edition, Sovereigh World Ltd., PO Box 777 4 on Bridge, Kent, TN 11 9XT, England, ISBN: 1-85240-039-0.

LaHaye, Tim Beverly. *El Acto Matrimonial*, edición 1976, Zondervan Corporations Grand Rapids, Michigan, 1976, impreso en Barcelona, España, pp. 30, 31, 124, 126, 196, 198. ISBN: 84-7228-269-4

Reina-Valera 1995 - Edición de Estudio, (Estados Unidos de América: Sociedades Bíblicas Unidas) 1998.

Strong James, LL.D, S.T.D., *Concordancia Strong Exhaustiva de la Biblia*, Editorial Caribe, Inc., Thomas Nelson, Inc., Publishers, Nashville, TN - Miami, FL, EE.UU., 2002. ISBN: 0-89922-382-6.

The New American Standard Version. Zordervan Publishing Company, ISBN: 0310903335.

The Tormont Webster's Illustrated Encyclopedic Dictionary. ©1990 Tormont Publications.

Vine, W.E. *Diccionario Expositivo de las Palabras del Antiguo Testamento y Nuevo Testamento*. Editorial Caribe, Inc./División Thomas Nelson, Inc., Nashville, TN, ISBN: 0899224954, 1999.

Ward, Lock A. *Nuevo Diccionario de la Biblia*. Editorial Unilit: Miami, Florida, ISBN: 07899-0217-6, 1999.

http://www.geocities.com/gusmatflo/elabusosexual

http://www.helpandhealing.org/AyudaParaVictimas.htm

http://www.fundaciontamar.net/Area%20Fisica/Abuso%20sexual/Que_es_el_abuso_sexual.htm

http://www.TopTenReviews.com/pornography

http://www.enough.org/

http://listas.eleconomista.es/economia/240-las-industrias-que-ms-dinero-mueven-en-el-mundo

http://www.uji.es/bin/publ/edicions/jfi9/publ/7.pdf

http://www.loveismore.es/menu2/estadisticas-pornografia.html

If this book has been a blessing for you, your family or your ministry, we would love for you to send us your comments. If you have a testimony of what the power of God has done in your life, you can call us at 305-382-3171, or write to us as:

kingjesusministry.org/share